WITHDRAWN. FO[...] [...] [...] IN CITY
CULTURAL AND WELFARE INSTITUTIONS
MAY BE SOLD FOR THE BENEFIT OF
THE NEW YORK PUBLIC LIBRARY ONLY.

SO-DVC-028

Puerto Rico

COMMONWEALTH, STATE,
OR NATION?

Puerto Rico

COMMONWEALTH, STATE, OR NATION?

By Byron Williams

Parents' Magazine Press • *New York*

Each Background Book is concerned with the broad spectrum of people, places, and events affecting the national and international scene. Written simply and clearly, the books in this series will engage the minds and interests of people living in a world of great change.

Library of Congress Cataloging in Publication Data

Williams, Byron, 1934-
    Puerto Rico: Commonwealth, state, or nation?

    Bibliography: p.
      1. Puerto Rico—History.   2. Puerto Rico—Relations
(general) with the United States.   3. U.S.—Relations
(general) with Puerto Rico.   I. Title.
F1971.W5   320.9'7295   79-183127
ISBN 0-8193-0573-1
ISBN 0-8193-0574-X (lib. bdg.)

Copyright © 1972 by Byron Williams
All rights reserved
Printed in the United States of America

CONTENTS

NB

DEC 1 1 1973

ACKNOWLEDGMENTS

The author and publisher are grateful for permission to quote from the following copyrighted material. (Specific page references for these quotes will be found in the *Notes*, which begin on page 233.)

Knox Burger Associates, Ltd. for Dan Wakefield's *Island in the City: The World of Spanish Harlem*. Boston: Houghton Mifflin Company, 1959.

Las Americas, Long Island City, N.Y. for José Luis Vivas's *The History of Puerto Rico*, 1970.

Praeger Publishers, Inc., New York, for Kal Wagenheim's *Puerto Rico: A Profile*, 1970.

1
BORIQUÉN AND TAÍNOS

THERE IS A common tendency to begin the story of
any American land with the "discovery" by Columbus in 1492, as if time had begun for these continents and islands with that event, but we can trace
the history of Puerto Rico back over some 185 million years to the time when the geographic system
of which it is a part began to take its present
shape. Before that, a vast, low plain extended
roughly from where Cuba is now almost to Mexico, and from Puerto Rico south to the South
American continent. Then the crust of the earth
was wracked powerfully and the Antillean Plain
sank under the waters of the Atlantic Ocean. Beyond the sunken land the earth's crust folded and
wrinkled and thrust a high mountain wall up out
of the sea. This wall, stretching from the American
mainland east toward Europe, broke up under the
pressures of earthquake and erosion and left the

1

four islands of the Greater Antilles: Cuba, Jamaica, Hispaniola (now Haiti and the Dominican Republic), and Puerto Rico. Each of the four is elongated on an east-west axis; except for Cuba, each has an east-west mountain spine that runs nearly its whole length.

To the east of Puerto Rico and curving south in an arc that reaches almost to the coast of Venezuela a chain of volcanic and coralline islands arose, known collectively as the Lesser Antilles. And so the geographic system commonly called the Caribbean was completed. Its principal element, the Caribbean Sea, flows where the Antillean Plain once was. It is bordered on the north by the Greater Antilles; on the east by the Lesser Antilles; on the west by the coasts of Mexico and Central America; and its southern border is formed by the coasts of Colombia and Venezuela.

Puerto Rico itself is 111 miles long and 36 miles wide and is surrounded by a shallow underwater shelf that varies in width from 2 to 7 miles. Three small offshore islands belong to Puerto Rico: Vieques, Culebra, and Mona. Altogether, Puerto Rico has a land area of 3,435 square miles, which makes it roughly the size of Connecticut. Its topography is dominated by its mountain spine, the Cordillera Central, the highest peak of which is Cerró de Punta—4,398 feet. The mountains and foothills account for three-fourths of Puerto Rico's land, yet there is great variety, ranging from coastal grasslands to rain forest to desert. Northeast tradewinds blow across the island, tempering the tropic's heat and discharging their moisture in heavy rainfall on the northern slopes. Rain is plentiful, though it varies in different parts of the island, and what doesn't soak into the soil returns to the sea via more than a thousand streams. No more than fifty of these streams are worthy of the name "river": the longest is less than fifty miles long; and none is navigable except by small boats.

Puerto Rico owes two particular features to its geographic location: earthquakes and hurricanes. The first are caused by geological faults in the sea floor near the island: in 1918 an earthquake caused tidal waves that combined with tremors to take 116 lives and destroy more than $4 million worth of property. Much more damage has been done to the island by hurricanes. Since written records of these storms began to be kept, in 1508, seventy-three have lashed the island. Long before Europeans intruded in the Caribbean these storms were recognized by Puerto Rico's inhabitants as one of nature's worst dangers. Our word "hurricane" comes from their *Juracán*, the god of evil, who caused the winds to rage when he was angry.

No one knows when the island's first settlers arrived, but archaeologists have found remains of an ancient culture they call the Archaics, who came into the Caribbean islands from the North American continent thousands of years ago. Traveling on log rafts, they came to Cuba first and then slowly spread their culture through the other islands until they had reached the Virgin Islands in the Lesser Antilles.

The Archaics left no traces of a technology. So far as is known today, they made no pots, built no houses, planted no crops. They banded together in small seminomadic groups and seem to have subsisted primarily on fish and shellfish.

After the Archaic culture, the Caribbean islands were invaded by another people, this time from the south—probably from the Orinoco River region of Venezuela. They were the Igneris, a subgroup of the Arawak culture, and they had developed a technology and culture that were much more advanced than that of the Archaics, though not to be compared with that of the Maya, Toltec, or Inca of the American mainland. On the other hand, the Igneris' island homes insulated them from the contacts and contests with neighbors that were part of the mainland civilizations' life. The Igneris were fishermen, sailors, and potters. Traveling in great canoes, they spread across the Caribbean islands all the way to Cuba. In the Virgin Islands or in Puerto Rico they met and dominated the Archaic people and settled down to live. Present-day knowledge of the Igneris is limited, but they left behind them clear evidence of their skills in pottery and ceramics. For their ceramic designs they had developed a palette of colors that included red, black, white, pink, and yellow. Land crabs were a favorite food—a preference that has lasted in Puerto Rico, though, in the twentieth century, waterfront expansion and pollution have made the crabs increasingly rare. Surely among the most significant of the Igneris' contributions to Puerto Rico and the Caribbean was the Arawak language which they introduced and which survived until after the European conquest. Europeans took many words from Arawak which are now part of the English and Spanish vocabularies. Most often, this happened when the Europeans found that the Native Americans (whom they called Indians) knew, made, or used an artifact, plant, or animal for which no word existed in the European languages. *Canoa,* the long slender craft that took the Igneris to sea, is still known, in English, as canoe.

But when the Igneris arrived in Puerto Rico the coming of the European was still in the future. After the Igneris had been on the island for some time they were succeeded by another culture, the Taíno. It is not clear whether the Taínos were another people, also of Arawak origin, who followed the Igneris into the islands from South America or whether the Taíno civilization was developed in the islands by descendants of the Igneris. In any event, the Taínos lived in a society that was technologically, agriculturally, socially, and philosophically more highly developed than that of the Igneris. As far as we know now, it was they who gave Puerto Rico its oldest name: they called their island Boriquén, or the Land of the Noble Lord.

The Taínos of Boriquén were of a dark copper

skin color, of medium height, and their hair was straight and dark. For aesthetic reasons, Taíno parents bound their children's heads in cotton wrappings to produce a back-sloping forehead. Their dress was simple: married women wore a cotton wrap called a *nagua*. From this Taíno word the Spaniards later developed the word *enaguas*, the Spanish word for slip or petticoat. Men, children, and unmarried women used no clothing. Men decorated their bodies with geometric designs painted in bright vegetable dyes, and when they went to battle they wore decorations of feathers in their hair and collars of stone or of animal teeth. Other decorations were of shells, clay, and gold.

The Taínos of Boriquén developed a highly organized social structure. As in Mexican and Incan society, it was based on a class system but was not nearly so elaborate as that of those mainland civilizations. The largest class, the *naborias*, provided most of the Taíno labor. Another class, the *nytainos*, supervised agriculture, trained young men in the arts of war, and kept order among the people. The *caciques*, or chieftains, were selected from among the *nytainos*. The third class, that of the *bohiques*, was made up of doctor-priests.

The Taínos were organized in tribes, each with its own settlement and fields as well as its own *cacique* and *bohique*. Over all the tribes of Boriquén was a Supreme Cacique whose title passed from father to son. If there was no heir, all of the island *caciques* would assemble and select a successor to the Supreme Cacique from among the sons of the dead chief's sisters.

Within each tribe the *bohique,* or doctor-priest, was the second most important personage. It was his responsibility to make offerings to the Supreme Being and Creator, *Yuquiyú,* and to appease the god of evil, *Juracán,* whose wrath could bring on the terrible storms we still call by his name. In order to speak with the gods and with lesser spirits the *bohique* would inhale powdered tobacco to assist him in entering a trance state. The stone effigy of *Yuquiyú,* as well as the *cemíes,* or stone symbols of minor spirits, were kept by the *bohique* in his role as priest. As doctor he was skilled in the uses of herbs and medicines and was responsible for the health of his people. It was he, too, who preserved in memory the tales of past heroes, of his people's history, and of the gods' teachings so that besides being doctor and priest he was also his tribe's living archive.

Taíno villages were small and were arranged on a common plan. A village's central feature was its *batey:* a plaza from which a straight street led out of the village, and where the Taínos held their religious ceremonies. There, the Taínos also had dances, sang, and played a ball game in which two teams competed, using heads, arms, and knees to keep a ball in the air. The team that allowed the ball to strike the ground lost the point.

Facing the *batey* was the *cacique*'s house, which

was built differently from any other in the village. Called a *caney*, it was rectangular and its walls were pierced by windows. At the front was a small balcony. Inside, its floors were made of planks hewn from palm trunks. Other houses in the village were of a type called *bohío:* circular houses of bamboo, roofs thatched with palm leaves, with only the doorway for ventilation. Floors were of earth and the one room in each house served as kitchen, dining room, and bedroom. Rather than crowding their *bohíos* together in the village, the Taínos preferred to space them out, giving the families breathing space. Inside, the *bohíos* were not crowded with furniture and objects: hammocks woven of cotton thread were swung from the roof beams for sleeping; three large stones made a fireplace in which a fire burned continually; stone or wooden seats provided places for the occupants to sit. On the walls hung *caratulas*, which were large clay masks of family ancestors. Clay was also used for making some of the kitchen utensils and storage pots. At the outer edge of the village the Taínos built lookout platforms in convenient trees from which they could guard the approaches to the village. A village might be located on the coast or near a stream, but water was always nearby—salt or fresh.

The principal occupation of the Taínos was agriculture. Without plows or draft animals that might have pulled them, they cultivated a large variety of crops, among which the most important were corn, tobacco, sweet potatoes, peanuts, yams, peppers, and a starchy root called *batata.* The principal agricultural tool was a pointed stick called *coa* with which the field workers made holes for planting. Besides the cultivated crops, a large variety of fruits and herbs that grew on the island were there for the gathering. Cotton, too, grew wild and its fibers were gathered and used without the necessity for cultivation.

Taíno craftsmen worked stone, of which they made hatchets and knives, religious objects and *dujos:* the low, high-backed seats that were an important part of the furniture of every *bohío.* Stonework went far beyond simple chipping: typical *cemíes* had a carved face at each end of an elongated stone. Between the two faces was the representation of a rising mountain.

Taíno mastery of pottery and ceramics was of a high order. Clay masks and *cemíes* were common. Pottery was usually decorated with figures of animal heads and multicolored geometric figures.

A third craft that was highly developed among the Taíno people was that of textiles. Though the Taínos used little clothing, they made use of both cotton and the fibers of the maguey from which they spun thread. Hammocks, fishing nets, fish lines, and *naguas* were the Taíno weavers' principal products. From native plants they made dyes of black and blue and yellow for textile decoration.

Hunting and fishing were important in the Taíno economy. Besides fishing with nets and with

hook-and-line, Taíno fishermen used certain nar-
cotic plants with which they could stun fish in
fresh-water streams. The drugged fish would float
to the surface where they could be easily gathered;
the fish that were not wanted on that day would
recuperate shortly and be available to be caught
another day. Birds and small animals were the
hunters' prey.

In the fifteenth century the Taíno population of
Boriquén was about thirty thousand people, divided among seventeen tribes. But time had not
stood still in the Americas since the Igneris began
their migration from Venezuela into the Caribbean islands. Even the most brief look at American
history in the fifteenth century reveals tremendous
forces at work among its peoples. In the Andean
and Pacific Coast regions of South America the
Inca Empire was at its height, but was soon to
know serious division and civil war. In the great
Valley of Mexico city-states maintained an uneasy
balance of power and an even less certain suprema-
cy over coastal civilizations. In the Yucatán the
clash of Maya and Toltec cultures culminated in a
series of bloody civil wars. And in the Caribbean
islands a new wave of South American people
were following the footsteps of Igneris north
through the Lesser Antilles.

These people were the Caribs, by whose name
the Europeans have come to know this entire system of sea and islands. They sailed large craft capable of holding up to a hundred men and were

probably the first to use sails in the Caribbean waters. Skillful as mariners and as warriors, they occupied the islands from Tobago to the Virgin Islands, and by the end of the fifteenth century they
were locked in struggle with the Taínos of Boriquén. Operating from nearby islands the Carib
piraguas would descend in sudden raids against the
coasts of Boriquén, and they often sailed away with
women and children captured in the raids. Ironically, it was a group of Taíno captives who, in order to escape their Carib captors, first led Europeans to Boriquén. The Europeans would soon
prove to be much more dangerous to the Taínos
than the Caribs were.

The Taínos of Boriquén were not the first Native Americans to meet men from Europe. In 1492
a small fleet of three ships had sailed into the Caribbean Sea from the Atlantic Ocean and had spent
some time sailing up and down the coasts of Cuba,
Jamaica, and Hispaniola. The fleet was an explora-
tory expedition authorized by the royal house of
Spain and was seeking an easy passage to India.
Commanded by Christopher Columbus, the expedition stopped along the island coasts from time to
time and sent landing parties ashore to make maps
of rivers and harbors and to take things: plants,
fruit, birds, gold nuggets, and a number of Native
Americans. When one of the three ships was
wrecked on the coast of Hispaniola the surviving
two ships sailed back to Spain. They left behind
them about forty European men to begin a Euro-

pean settlement on Hispaniola, where Taíno *caciques* had received them with consideration.

Back in Spain, Columbus reported the success of his expedition. He had reached the Indias, he said, and he produced his captured "Indians" to prove it. He also produced his gold samples. Pleased, the king and queen of Spain authorized a second and larger expedition to return to "India" and to set about the business of colonizing it: that is, of bringing its lands and people under subjection of the Spanish Crown and the Catholic Church, and its gold into the Spanish treasury. Seventeen ships were made ready: stores for the colony were put aboard; map makers and astronomers were recruited; soldiers, laborers, and artisans (some of them criminals who received pardons on condition that they become colonists abroad) were procured for the expedition. All in all, 1,200 men sailed from Spain on September 25, 1493, to make "India" a dependency of Spain. Actually, it was the beginning of Europe's conquest of two continents and their adjacent island systems, and the beginning of the end of long centuries of American civilization.

On November 3, 1493, this second fleet sailed into the Caribbean Sea, entering through the Lesser Antilles, which were now in the possession of the Caribs. A few days later, on the island the Spaniards renamed Santa María de Guadalupe, twelve Taíno women and two boys who had been taken prisoner in one of the Carib raids against Boriquén met with a Spanish shore party. By this time some of Columbus's earlier captives had learned the Spanish language and had been pressed into service as interpreters. They explained the Taínos' predicament to the Spanish, and the women and boys were taken aboard the Spanish ships. On November 19 the Spanish fleet sailed near the coast of a large and lovely island: Boriquén. The women and children rescued from the Caribs did not wait to be put ashore. Perhaps, by that time, they had learned enough about their benefactors to be uncertain that they would be put ashore. In any event, they jumped overboard and swam for the island. Columbus continued along the coast until he reached a bay where the fleet stopped for two days, taking on water, gathering fruits, and catching fish. Columbus left an account of that first European visit to Boriquén which was paraphrased by Fray Bartolomé de las Casas a few years later in his *Historia de las Indias*. Among other things, Columbus described:

> . . . some houses that were very artfully made, although of straw and wood; and there was a plaza, with a road leading to the sea, very clean and straight, made like a street, and the walls were of crossed or woven cane; and above, beautiful gardens, as if they were vineyards or orchards or citron trees, such as there are in Valencia or Barcelona; and next to the sea was a high watchtower, where ten or twelve people could fit, also well made; it must have been the pleasure-house of the lord of that island; or of that part of the island.[1]

It was no lord's pleasure-house that Columbus had found but one of the *yucayeques* of the Taíno people. Columbus renamed the island San Juan Bautista and sailed off with his fleet, anxious to return to Boriquén's neighboring island (already renamed Hispaniola by Columbus), where the first Spanish colonizers had been left behind the year before. For a few more years Boriquén remained free of Europeans and its people continued to be occupied with their own lives and with the defense of their island against continuing Carib attacks.

Columbus found that all of the Spaniards he had left on Hispaniola had been killed. Though the people of the island had received them with courtesy, continued abuses by the Spaniards— particularly their abuses of the island women—had eventually produced a violent retaliation. Every last Spaniard was killed. Columbus and his 1,200 colonists came ashore and settled down: this time without the cooperation of the people they called Indians. But the Spaniards had horses, armor, trained war dogs, steel weapons, and guns. They had learned the disciplines of warfare during hundreds of years of violent struggle against the Moors in Spain. And in spite of resistance on Hispaniola they were able to force their intrusion, ship hundreds of Indians back to Spain to be sold as slaves, and enforce a system of slave labor among the Indians whom they forced to dig for gold and to till the fields, all for the benefit of Spain. In 1496 the Spaniards founded the first European city in America and named it Santo Domingo. For years it was to remain the center of Spanish government in the Americas.

Boriquén was not revisited by Spaniards until the year 1499 when Vicente Yañez Pinzón, a sea captain who had sailed from Hispaniola to explore the continent to the south, stopped at the island on his way back to Spain. On Boriquén he found what he thought was evidence of much wealth in gold. In Spain he showed his gold samples and obtained the king's authorization to colonize the island. To prepare the way, Pinzón sent a shipload of pigs and goats to be turned loose on Boriquén. But he himself was fated never to return to the island; in 1508 he sold his rights to colonize to Martín García de Salazar. Already it was clear that, to the Europeans, Indians and their lands were no more than property that could be passed from hand to hand like so many pounds of cheese. Martín García de Salazar, however, profited little from his purchase. By the time he was ready to "take up his rights," the Spanish governor of Hispaniola had rewarded a soldier by the name of Juan Ponce de León for his good services in the fight against Hispaniola's Indians by permitting him to take charge of an expedition to colonize Boriquén. On August 12, 1508, Ponce de León sailed from Hispaniola with a company of fifty men.

Agueybana the Elder, *cacique* of Guaynía and Supreme Cacique of Boriquén received Ponce de León in a conference that the Puerto Rican historian Professor Lidio Cruz Monclova has called "an act of cordial coexistence, rather than one of territorial surrender. . . ."[2] The cordiality, at least on the part of Agueybana, is evident in that the *ca-cique* received the Spanish chief with a solemn Taíno ritual of friendship. Agueybana exchanged names with Juan Ponce de León. Then he helped the Spaniard in his search for gold and for a convenient place to begin Spanish settlement. On the north coast of the island Ponce de León found a beautiful natural harbor to which he gave the name Puerto Rico. Nearby there was a river called the Toa in whose stream-bed were nuggets of gold. On the banks of the Toa the Spaniards set up some shacks and began washing gold from the river. Also, with the help of Taíno labor provided by Agueybana, a sort of agricultural experiment station was set up so that the colonizers could learn to plant and cultivate native crops. A little farther to the northeast they built a stone house, beginning the first permanent European town in the island: Caparra.

Ponce de León's expedition also introduced Taínos of Boriquén and Africans to each other. Juan Garrido was a Black man who had been a slave in Spain; through his own efforts he had purchased his freedom and then made his way to Hispaniola. When Ponce de León sailed to colonize Boriquén, Juan Garrido joined the expedition. Though there is evidence that Africans had reached the Americas in times preceding Columbus's voyage, Juan Garrido apparently was the first Black man to reach Boriquén. Since 1501 Spain had been granting licenses for the importation of

Black slaves to Hispaniola. Though there is no concrete evidence that this is so, it is most likely that Black slaves were brought to Puerto Rico as early as 1509, when Ponce de León brought more settlers, with their families and dependents, from Hispaniola. Juan Garrido later took part in Ponce de León's expedition to Florida and so may have been the first Black man to set foot on North American soil. Still later Juan Garrido was a member of the expedition led by Hernan Cortéz against Mexico. Cortéz was the first European to destroy a Native American civilization; Juan Garrido was the first man ever to plant wheat on the American mainland.

2

BORIQUÉN BECOMES PUERTO RICO

IN BOOKS THAT treat of the transplanting of European culture to the Americas one often reads that white men were mistaken for gods by Native Americans, as, for example, by the Taínos of Boriquén. The inference seems to be that Native Americans were so impressed by the horses and armor and guns of the European newcomers that they could account for them only by ascribing them to the supernatural. If this is so, perhaps it will help to keep things in perspective to recall that white Europeans were by no means immune to such superstitious reasoning themselves. For example, when a white man in Europe had invented a telescope some years before, many of his fellows denounced the instrument as an evil and supernatural device—and Galileo was imprisoned for reporting what he saw through it. And about a hundred and fifty years after white people came to America. English colonists in Massachusetts burned people alive for supposedly keeping company with the devil.

But there is another factor that was involved in the Taínos' and other Native Americans' belief that Spaniards were more than natural men. And that is that the Spaniards claimed to be gods and immortal in order to command obedience from people whose lands and lives they were violating. In Boriquén, in the other Caribbean islands, and in Florida it was a common ploy of the *conquistador*. During De Soto's expedition into North America, for example, his men were so conscious that their lives depended on the Native Americans' belief in their immortality that when De Soto died his soldiers concealed the fact and buried his body secretly. In Boriquén, Ponce de León used the same ruse, telling the Taínos that Spaniards were superior beings who could not die or be killed. Spaniards found a rationalization for themselves, of course, by which they could maintain that they were not lying. After all, St. John had written that "to them gave He power to become the sons of God, even to those who believed on his name." And the promise of eternal life was an essential element of Spaniards' official religion.

In the early days of the Spanish presence in Boriquén, relations between them and the Taínos were fairly pleasant and were fostered by the principal *cacique*, Agueybana, whose cordial reception of Ponce de León was described in the preceding

chapter. Agueybana seemed well disposed to accept the Spaniards' claims as to their origin and
their object in coming to the island. Their object,
as the Spaniards explained it, was to teach the
Taíno people the true religion and a better way of
life. In order to accomplish this, they said, each
Spanish settler would take a group of Taíno people under his personal care. That the Spaniards
themselves were not under any illusions about
what they were doing is clear from the term they
used for this system by which they made slaves of
the Taínos; they called it quite plainly the *reparti-
miento,* or distribution. Taínos, far from entering on
a better life, found themselves digging for gold
and tending Spaniards' fields under brutal working conditions. They found themselves subject to
Spaniards' rules on their own island, and were
severely punished for any infraction of the rules.
Taíno women were taken at will by those Spaniards
who had come to America alone, as most had, and
this contributed greatly to a growing hatred of the
white intruders. Though Agueybana honored his
pledge of friendship, his brother Guaybaná—who
was "distributed" to Ponce de León's second in
command, Cristóbal de Sotomayor—developed an
implacable hatred of the Spaniards and became the
principal leader in the inevitable Taíno rebellion.

Matters were made worse for the Taínos when a
conflict arose among the Spaniards themselves as
to who was to rule Boriquén, or San Juan as the
Spaniards called the island at that time. Ponce de

León had been appointed to colonize and govern by Nicolás de Ovando, governor of Hispaniola. But in 1509 Ovando's position was taken from him by the Spanish government and given to Diego Colón, heir of Christopher Columbus. In spite of explicit instructions from the king that he was to respect the appointment of Ponce de León, Colón had no sooner arrived in Hispaniola than he appointed a friend, Juan Cerón, to govern San Juan (Boriquén). The arbitrariness of his *repartimientos* of Taínos among his own followers from Hispaniola angered the Taínos and the earlier Spanish settlers as well. Ponce de León had received his authority from the king, who had named him Captain General; so Ponce de León's lieutenant, Sotomayor, took matters into his own hands. He took Cerón by surprise and shipped him back to Spain as a prisoner. Cerón's rule had been short, but his exceptionally high-handed treatment of the Taínos had added fuel to an already smoldering fire of Taíno hatred. When Agueybana died and Guaybaná took his place as Supreme Cacique of the Taínos of Boriquén, only the lingering fear of the Spaniards' supposed immortality prevented a general revolt.

But the Spanish claim of immortality could not be maintained forever. In the year 1510, the Taínos freed themselves of that belief once and for all, and opened the way for a determined resistance against Spanish domination. (Ironically, 1510 was also the year in which the Spaniards first smelted the nuggets mined for them by Taíno labor and had the pleasure of seeing them transformed into shining gold ingots worth some hundred thousand pesos.) Though they were ultimately defeated by European disease, hunger, and superior weapons, once they had established for themselves that Spaniards were men and not gods, the Taínos proved they were more than willing to match themselves against the Spanish. In fact, it was because of a Taíno's willingness to challenge a Spaniard's presumed divinity that the myth of immortality was broken.

Near the western end of the island was the *yucayeque* of Yagueca, near a river called the Guaorabo then and Grande de Añasco today. A young Spaniard, Diego Salcedo, showed up there one day. He told the *cacique*, Urayoán, that he was just passing through and asked for a few Taíno men to carry his gear and to serve as guides. Urayoán had lived for a long time; he had serious doubts about the Spaniards' claim to immortality. So, before sending the guides off with Salcedo, Urayoán spoke privately to them. When the party reached the Guaorabo River, Salcedo ordered his guides to carry him over so that he would not wet his clothes. They obeyed, but in the middle of the stream they switched from obeying his orders to obeying those of their *cacique*, Urayoán, and dumped Salcedo into the water. Then they held him under. Some measure of the extent to which the Spaniards had implanted the notion of their immortality is revealed by the fact that those Taíno men held Salcedo underwater for several hours before dragging his body to the bank. Even then, though obviously as dead as any mortal can be, they took no chances. Another white man, they had been told, had lain in a tomb for three days before demonstrating his immortality, so for three days they watched over Salcedo's corpse until its deteriorating condition removed the last possible vestige of doubt. News of this event ran from one end of the island to the other: the Spaniards were not gods; they were men; they could die and bloat and rot like any other men. And as the message spread, so did plans for war against the Spanish intruders.

Spaniards had been on the island only about two years, but they had already made a beginning at undercover work. Juan González, a Spaniard who had learned the Arawak language, spent a lot of time disguised as a Taíno and listening to their talk. He brought word to Sotomayor that trouble was brewing near the settlement that Sotomayor had founded and named after himself on the northwest coast near present-day Aguada. When he received the news from González, Sotomayor was on the south coast of the island, near the home seat of Guaybaná. He decided to march his men back to Villa de Sotomayor, and told Guaybaná that he was going. They had been on the march only a few hours when they were attacked by Taíno warriors led by Guaybaná. The attack was successful; Sotomayor's party was killed almost to a man. Shortly afterward, a Taíno force attacked the Villa de Sotomayor. They were led this time by the *cacique* Guarionex, and again the Taínos were successful. The town was destroyed and only a few survivors managed to reach Caparra with the news that the Taínos had declared war.

Ponce de León was a veteran of the fighting in Hispaniola, as were many of his men at Caparra. Whatever else might be said of those Spaniards, no one could accuse them of cowardice in battle. Having decided to strike the gathering Taíno force by surprise, Ponce de León led one hundred and twenty-five men in a forced march across the Cordillera Central and came upon the Taíno camp during the night. It is reported that there were six thousand Taínos in camp that night. After they were asleep Ponce de León led a screaming charge into the camp. Taken by surprise, the Taínos were unable to rally. They fled, leaving more than two hundred dead behind. Not a single Spaniard was killed in that fight.

Smaller battles, bloody and fiercely fought, followed. Then, in the region of Yagueca, where Spanish mortality had first been proved, Guaybaná gathered his forces to strike a final crushing blow at Ponce de León. This time the Spaniards were on the defensive, entrenched behind breastworks of felled trees at the top of a hill. From their fortified position the Spaniards kept up a gunfire that was capable of intimidating the Taínos far beyond its actual ability to do them damage. As the fighting progressed, however, the Taínos began to get over their fear of the Spaniards' gunfire. They pressed closer and closer, and it seemed inevitable that the Spanish position would be overrun. But then a shot from a Spanish gun struck and killed Guaybaná. For the moment, it seems that funeral duties to their Supreme Cacique were more important to the Taíno warriors than the lives of Ponce de León and his men: carrying Guaybaná's body with them, the Taínos withdrew from the field. Ponce de León led his men back to the safety of Caparra and from there sent out messages offering amnesty to all "rebels" who would lay down their arms and agree to live in peace.

Although major Taíno resistance ended for a time with Guaybaná's death, only a minority of the Indians accepted Ponce de León's amnesty. Two of the island *caciques* agreed to peace, but the rest, and most of their people, either took refuge in remote mountain regions (where later they would be joined by escaped Black slaves) or fled the island in their canoes to seek refuge on neighboring islands. Many others, unable to escape and unwilling to endure servitude, killed their children and committed suicide themselves. Faced with the loss of their labor supply, the Spaniards became hunters, tracking Taínos through the mountains and forcing them to accept "distribution." Ponce de León appealed to the king for a ship with which to pursue the Taínos who escaped by sea. Sporadic clashes between Spaniard and Taíno continued to occur, but the death of Guaybaná marked the end of Taíno dominion in their own land. From 1511 on there was no doubt that the Spaniards were in control, and Boriquén had become San Juan.

There remained, however, the question of just which Spaniard was to be in command. Unlike the Taínos, the Spaniards on the island could not simply choose who could best govern them. The supposedly "more advanced" Spaniards were not free to do so; they were subjects of the Spanish king, who ruled over them by Divine Right. All authority, therefore, came down from above and men who sought authority had to seek it in the favor of those more powerful than themselves. Both Ponce de León and Juan Cerón wanted the honor of governing the new colony of San Juan. Ponce de León claimed his right to do so by favor of the king, Juan Cerón claimed it by favor of Diego Colón, governor of Hispaniola and of all the Indies. As has been described, that struggle was temporarily decided before the great Taíno revolt when Ponce de León's lieutenant, Sotomayor, arrested Cerón and shipped him back to Spain. Once there, of course, Cerón had hastened to press the justice of his claim before the Court.

In 1511 the king's Royal Council decided that the right to name governors in new American colonies belonged to the governor of the Indies and not to the king. Ponce de León, therefore, was declared in the wrong and the governorship of San

Juan was returned to Juan Cerón. In November of
that same year, Cerón returned to the island and
Ponce de León surrendered his office. Now unemployed, he set off in search of a fabulous place he
had heard of, called Bimini, where there was supposed to be a fountain that would make anyone
who bathed in its waters young forever. If such a
fountain existed, or exists, it has yet to be found.
Ponce de León did reach Florida, though, and
claimed it for the king of Spain.

The squabble between Ponce de León and Cerón was not the first of its sort that the king and his
Royal Council had had to settle, nor would it be
the last. But it helped to make clear in Spain the
need for a better structure through which the will
of Spain and its king could be executed in the new
colonies and through which authority might more
efficiently flow downward from king and government to the least of their American subjects. Since
the system established by Spain was to affect the
island of San Juan (soon to change its name yet
again to Puerto Rico) for nearly four hundred
years, it is worth outlining at least its broader
forms.

Still in the year 1511, a Council of the Indies
was formed in Spain, made up of Spanish noblemen and high church officials. Formed initially as
an advisory body to the king, in a few years it became the supreme authority of political and economic administration for the Spanish colonies in
America. It was this body that passed laws for

America and sat as a Supreme Court of appeal for disputes arising in the colonies. All matters of shipping, commerce, and trade between the colonies, and between the colonies and Spain, were decided by the *Casa de Contratación*, a special body set up for that purpose by the Council of the Indies. The *Casa* exercised a strict monopoly of trade with the colonies in order to insure that its profits remained in the hands of the king and, of course, in the hands of a select group of Spanish businessmen who were able to gain control of the *Casa*. All trade between Spain and its American colonies had to be handled through Seville; in America, only Veracruz (Mexico), Cartagena (Colombia), and Puerto Bello (Panama) were ports of free trade. All goods going to America from Spain and vice versa had to be passed through by the *Casa de Contratación*. This body not only controlled the tax revenues of all trade, but could decide what goods could be traded, how much could be charged for them, and who could provide them. The opportunities for exploitation, profiteering, and corruption inherent in such a monopoly system are obvious. None of those opportunities was wasted.

Under the Council of Indies an administrative system within the colonies was created. In place of a governor of the Indies, with authority over all of Spain's American colonies, it was found preferable to divide the colonies into Viceroyalties and Captaincies General. Captains general were responsible to the viceroys; viceroys were responsible to the king. The first Viceroyalty created was that of New Spain (Mexico). Later, the Viceroyalties of Peru, of New Granada (Colombia), and of La Plata (Argentina, Bolivia, Uruguay, and Paraguay) were formed. The Captaincy General of Guatemala included all of Central America except Panama. Chile and Venezuela were each established as Captaincies General, while that of Cuba included Florida, Cuba, and San Juan (Puerto Rico).

Viceroys and captains general were executive and military authorities. Justice in many matters was also administered in their districts by these officials, but they could be challenged before *Audiencias* which were high tribunals, whose judges were called *oidores*, or hearers, and were the only legal bodies in America that could oppose or limit the power of viceroys. The first *Audiencia* was established in Hispaniola, with jurisdiction over the Antilles and Venezuela.

At the local level, the basic unit of government in the Spanish colonies was the municipality. The governing body was the *Cabildo*, composed of a citizens' council and presided over by a regional governor. The *Cabildo* of Caparra was organized in 1511, but in November the town's name was officially changed to Puerto Rico, and it was given its coat of arms. This was the first coat of arms granted by the Spanish Crown to an American colony.

By 1514 the towns of San Germán and Santiago had been established. But if the number of Spanish colonists in the island was increasing, the oppo-

site was true of the Taínos. In that same year a
census showed that there were fewer than four
thousand Indians on the island, and these were no
happier with the Spaniards than Guaybaná had
been. A new rebellion broke out and Taínos attacked and burned the new settlement of Santiago.
Led by the *cacicque* Cacimar, Taíno warriors went
on to face the Spanish soldiers led by the then-
governor Mendoza. After a stubborn battle the
Taínos were defeated when Cacimar was killed,
recalling the death of Guaybaná and the last-min-
ute defeat of the forces he led. Mendoza followed
up his advantage by embarking his men in Taíno
canoes and Spanish boats and carrying the attack
to the dependent islet of Vieques, where Cacimar's
brother, Yaureibo, had gathered a force of Taínos
in exile. Yaureibo was killed in the fight that followed; his forces, too, were defeated by the Spaniards. Faced with a drastically dwindling labor
supply and disappointed in their expectation of
easy gold, Spanish colonists increased their requests for Black slaves to be admitted to the island.
Colonists' interest in San Juan lost its vigor.

Also, after the first rush of conquest by Spanish
soldiers, there were Spaniards whose humanity
revolted at the inhuman treatment dealt to the
Taínos. In Hispaniola and Cuba the Dominicans
Fray Antonio de Montesino and Fray Bartolomé de
las Casas preached against Spanish injustice and
cruelty to the Indians, and they carried their message to Spain where, separately, they argued their

convictions before the king and the most influential clergymen of the realm. They were successful — at least to the extent of obtaining an edict that defined Indians as freemen, specified the obligations of Spaniards toward the Indians "distributed" to their care, and limited the conditions of labor. But as was to happen again and again in the history of Spanish colonization, it proved much easier for idealistic clergymen and noblemen in Spain to issue edicts than it was for Spanish colonists to obey them. When, in 1521, all Indians "distributed" to work lands and mines belonging to the Crown were ordered set free, along with those "distributed" to persons who did not live on the island, only some six hundred Taínos were found eligible. Nor were they in fact set free; they were taken to the farm originally set up by Ponce de León on the Toa River and put to work in agriculture. By this time the experimental farm was busy experimenting with European crops introduced to the island. Hopes of gold were dying; agriculture seemed the only alternative for the island.

In 1521, too, the town of Puerto Rico was moved from its location on the bay and reestablished on a small island in the bay. Town and island changed names: what had been the town of Puerto Rico became the town of San Juan; what had been the island of San Juan became the island of Puerto Rico. The island's name would not change again until the twentieth century when it passed from Spain's control into the hands of the United States and became, for about thirty years, Porto Rico.

Fifteen years after Ponce de León's invasion of the island, the basic conditions of Puerto Rican colonial life as it was to develop began to be apparent. The future hardly seemed bright to the Spaniards who had wrested possession of the island from the Taínos. They had come for gold, excited by the nuggets found in the island's riverbeds. Assuming that the river gold was evidence of rich deposits buried somewhere beneath the earth, the Spaniards almost destroyed an entire people in a few years' search for treasure. But there were no big deposits; the gold washed by centuries of rainfall into the island streams was quickly exhausted. Colonists, busy with hunting gold and with subduing Taínos, certain that any day they would become suddenly rich, went further and further into debt to the merchants who monopolized the supply of flour, oil, wine, clothing, and manufactured goods brought from Spain. As Black slaves became more and more important to the gold-seekers as replacements for the Taínos, the colonists' debt increased. Black slaves had to be purchased: the demand for them in the island was great, but the money to buy them was scarce. Spaniards went into debt to buy slaves, then pledged their slaves to borrow money for necessities, and had to give their slaves into the care of the lender in order to guarantee the loans' security. So they were again

without the slave labor they considered necessary
in order to find the gold that would pay for their
original indebtedness. Caught in this circle, many
were imprisoned for debt; others followed the
example of the Taínos themselves and fled into
the mountains where they learned to live off the
land and became hunters of the wild cattle de-
scended from the free-running first herds introduced by Spaniards.

Others found in agriculture some hope to take
the place of their vanished dreams of gold. Sugar
cane, introduced in the earliest years of the invasion, proved to do very well at the experimental
farm at Toa. Sugar was not gold, but like gold it
represented an article of value that could be sold
to the outside world. In 1523 Tomás de Castellón
set up the first sugar mill near San Germán, thus
beginning an industry that has been a major—and
often crucial—factor in the life of Puerto Rico until
this day. But if sugar promised the Spaniards a
new reason for remaining on the island, it also
insured that they would increase their demand for
slave labor, for the cultivation and processing of
sugar cane demanded large amounts of arduous
labor. As in the other Caribbean islands, sugar and
Black slavery went hand in hand in Puerto Rico.

Puerto Rico did not boom overnight as a flour-
ishing sugar economy. Far from it.

Spanish adventurers' disappointment at finding
so little gold was made even more acute by news of
the incredible wealth that their compatriots were

stealing from the people of Mexico and South America. That news produced strong reactions among other European nations as well, and ships sailed from France and from England to challenge Spain's exclusive right to the profits obtained from the looting of the American peoples. Soon, the continuing raids against Puerto Rico by the Caribs were supplemented by raids of French and English pirates. Since sugar cane was grown on the narrow coastal plains most vulnerable to attack, these raids did nothing to encourage the development of that industry. Smallpox, too, struck the island in an epidemic that took the lives of many Spaniards and was felt even more disastrously among the remaining Taínos. Then, in one year, three hurricanes devastated the island.

It seems no wonder that the most fervent prayer of the colonists came to be "¡Dios me lleve al Perú¡" ("God take me to Peru!"). It became almost impossible to keep them on the island and for a while it seemed as if the invasion of Boriquén and the annihilation of its people had been for nothing; that the wave of European invaders would simply roll on and leave the now depopulated island.

However, even though the island had lost its importance to fortune-seeking Spanish adventurers, the growing struggle with other European powers for possession of the Caribbean and America made the island more important to Spain because of its strategic location. Spain decreed the death penalty for any colonist caught trying to flee the island; some efforts were made to provide loans and supplies of Black slaves to encourage the sugar industry; soldiers were stationed on the island and forts were begun to insure that the island remained in Spanish hands. Spain's attempts to keep possession of Puerto Rico were successful; its flag continued to fly over the island for another three hundred and fifty years and more.

More than anything else, it was the determination by Spain to keep Puerto Rico as a military stronghold that shaped the island's history, while its agricultural development and trade took a secondary place. In the daily lives of its people, however, the situation was reversed, for people live by bread rather than by policy. Spanish military and political policy required a Spanish Puerto Rico; the people in Puerto Rico — Taíno, Spanish, and African — required food, clothing, houses, tools, schools, doctors, churches, and social organization. With agriculture as their principal resource, and within the limits of narrow restrictions imposed by the mother country of Spain, the people of Puerto Rico began the work that would in time create a Puerto Rican people.

The transition from gold-hunting get-rich-quick adventuring to culture-building took place over several years, of course, but the year 1530 seems a convenient one to mark the start of the new phase that was to last until the beginning of the nineteenth century. For one thing, in 1530 a census was taken on the island. Also, by that year the basic decision not to permit the Spanish colony to vanish had been made, as well as the decision to foster sugar production as a resource. Puerto Rican colonists' requests for more, and cheaper, slave labor had been recognized by Spain as valid; attempts were being made by Spain to control the importation of slaves so as to maintain a "safe" racial balance and to protect the Spanish government's right to profit from that trade by selling licenses and imposing taxes. Also by 1530 the practice of contraband trading (principally in slaves) had become enough of a reality to provoke strong countermeasures by the government. Contraband — one result of legal commercial monopoly and its attempts to keep exclusive control of the profits that were to be made from supplying Puerto Rico's needs and from taking Puerto Rico's products — was to continue as a fact of Puerto Rican life during all of its colonial relationship to Spain.

1530: On the whole island there were 327 white persons, 2,292 Black slaves, and somewhat more than 1,000 Taínos. In San Juan there were about 120 houses, some of stone but most of wood and thatch. Puerto Rico's first bishop, Alonso Manso, was on the island and under his direction a church was under construction in San Juan. There was also a Dominican monastery, begun in 1523. The military fortifications that were to make San Juan so formidable to the French, the English, and the Dutch had not yet been built. Of the other Spanish settlements begun on the island, San Germán had been burned by Caribs two years earlier and Santiago had been destroyed in the second Taíno rebellion, as Villa de Sotomayor had been in the first. Caribs continued to attack the Spaniards. Just the year before (October 18, 1529) eight Carib boats had entered San Juan harbor and captured a ferryboat with its load of Spaniards and Black slaves. The Caribs very nearly managed to get out of the harbor safely, but a lucky cannon shot killed a number of Carib warriors and three of their Black prisoners. And on October 23, 1530, Carib raiders at the Daguao plantation of Cristóbal de Guzmán destroyed the plantation, killed a number of its defenders, and captured twenty-five Black prisoners.

In 1530 Spain held Puerto Rico, though its work of colony-building had just begun. The seed of what was to become the Puerto Rican people had not yet sprouted, but it had been planted.

3
BIRTH OF A PEOPLE

IT HAS BEEN pointed out by Gordon K. Lewis in *Puerto Rico: Freedom and Power in the Caribbean* that "when in 1898 the Puerto Rican people passed to the suzerainty of the United States of America, they were confronted with unrelieved ignorance on the part of their new masters concerning the island territory and its history."[1] Since 1898 a large number of books and studies have been produced in an effort to relieve the ignorance that Lewis noted. These very books have repeatedly given false information about the island and the lies have become so standard as to seem axiomatic. For example, there is the repeated assertion that Puerto Rico has no exploitable natural resources other than the agricultural capacity of its soil, although today United States industry is busy mining copper on the island. Or the common assertion that between the time of the initial conquest of

Boriquén by Spain and the conquest of Spanish
Puerto Rico by the United States Army, nothing of
any interest or importance happened on the island. It is true that Puerto Rico does not have an
"interesting" history of war and aggression during
this period: Puerto Rico conquered no other land
or people; it never became the battlefield of flam-
boyant struggle, with the march and counter-
march of armies to stir the imagination of later-
day novelists and moviemakers.

All the same, even militarily, Puerto Rico has a
definite and distinctive history. Puerto Rico fought
no revolutionary war for its independence (which
is unique enough to be interesting in itself), yet it
played a role in many of the American wars for
independence, including the one fought by the
thirteen British colonies of North America. No
fantastic wealth was discovered in Puerto Rico to
dazzle historians, yet as early as the seventeenth
century New York pirates found Puerto Rican
towns worth raiding. Puerto Rico had no spectacular flooding of immigrants to liven its history.
Many of its Spanish settlers came and stayed on
the island reluctantly; most of its Black people
came in chains. Yet in the course of several
hundred years Puerto Rico developed a population larger than that of some other American nations and a people as distinctive as any in the
world.

As has been mentioned, it was Puerto Rico's
strategic position in the Caribbean, rather than its

wealth, that made it important to Spain. Europe
was a ferment of religious and political jealousies
and aspirations, and in Europe Spain was a swiftly
growing national power: proud, Catholic, and to
be reckoned with. Spain claimed exclusive rights
to all of both American continents and their island
dependencies—except for the tip of South America's eastward-reaching bulge that accidentally fell
to Portugal. And when the tales of American
wealth reached the ears of Englishmen and
Frenchmen already jealous and fearful of Spain's
growing European power, it was more than some
of them could endure. While England and Spain
jockeyed on the edge of war, English seamen raided Spanish shipping and Spanish settlements in
America. French Huguenots, fleeing a religious
civil war at home in which Spain sided against
them, sailed to His Most Catholic Majesty's American possessions and founded settlements in Florida. Spanish forces raided the French; the French
struck back by turning pirate. So even before the
English-Spanish war at the end of the sixteenth
century, Spain's colonies felt the effects of Spain's
European animosities: as witness the French take-
over of the islet of Mona in 1521, from which they
raided Spanish shipping. In 1528 they attacked San
Germán, sacking and burning it. From 1538 to
1544 they repeated their attacks a number of times.
The Treaty of Crespy, which was meant to resolve
the problems between France and Spain in 1544 interrupted the French attacks on Puerto Rico, but

new hostilities in Europe brought renewed French attacks after 1552. The last French attacks on San Germán in the sixteenth century (1571 and 1576) were disastrous for the French. Few as the Spanish, Indian, and African inhabitants of Puerto Rico were, by then they had learned at least to rely on each other in the fight against outside aggressors.

They could not rely on themselves, however, for the ammunition that a continuing defense of the island required. Gunpowder, guns, and steel all had to come from Spain and were expensive. To answer the big guns carried by the warships and armed merchant ships with which Puerto Rico's European enemies attacked its coasts, big guns were needed on the island, as well as fortifications in which to mount them. All of these things were beyond the means of the colonists, so it became the responsibility of the Spanish king and the Spanish government to provide for the defense of Puerto Rico. In 1533 the Spanish Crown's decision to fortify Puerto Rico resulted in construction being started on the Fortaleza in San Juan. A few years later, in 1539, work was begun on the fortification of the promontory that commands the entrance to the bay of San Juan: the huge El Morro castle that still attracts so many visitors to San Juan. Work on a fortress for the protection of San Germán was begun in 1541.

In Puerto Rico, the principal investment of funds was for the construction of fortifications and for the purchase of armaments. Initially, the capital necessary for fortifying the island was supplied by the Spanish Crown; later by the Viceroyalty of New Spain (Mexico). Probably most of such money was spent in Spain for iron hoops, swords, guns, steel, gunpowder, lead, medicines, oil, grease, and so forth, that were to be used in Puerto Rico. That part of the funds that reached the island for the maintenance of troops, payment of troop salaries, and support of the island government found its way back to the merchant houses of Spain through their agents in the island. Flour, olive oil, wax, and wine were some of the everyday items that Spaniards in Puerto Rico found necessary for life as they knew it, which had to be imported under a system of trading monopoly and awkward sea communication.

Development of Puerto Rico took place slowly. Faced with piracy on the seas, Spain developed the fleet system under which all ships sailing for America gathered into large convoys that were then escorted across the Atlantic by Spanish warships. The same system was used for bringing the produce and treasure of America back to Spain. Added to the extremely rigid trade restrictions already in effect, the fleet system further limited communication between Spain and its American colonies, though it helped to guarantee the profits of Spanish merchant houses favored with licenses to trade overseas.

The Spanish Crown did recognize, to some extent, the need of Puerto Rico's colonists to be

able to earn a cash income in order to pay for
goods they could not themselves produce. As early
as 1536 the Crown pardoned all debts of those
engaged in growing sugar. Later, slaves, tools, and
supplies necessary to produce sugar were made
exempt from foreclosure. Both these measures
point up the stranglehold on agricultural production that Spanish merchants held in the island,
since they were practically the only source of credit. To further ease the credit problem in order to
stimulate sugar production, the Crown also authorized a sum for direct loans to finance the
construction of sugar mills. These measures had
good initial results, and sugar production began to
climb.

As Spain's decision to fortify the city of San Juan
provided a cornerstone for an urban development
in Puerto Rico, so sugar provided the first truly
productive basis for rural development. The two
developments were distinct and were formed by
distinct conditions, yet the two were linked insep-
arably, though unequally, by rural dependence
on urban power. The money that came into the
island came through San Juan, either as funds for
military and governmental construction and support, or as the proceeds from Puerto Rican goods
sold in Spain by San Juan's merchants. Some of
the military funds found their way into the countryside to pay for local produce purchased for the
military garrison or for the slaves working on fortifications. Some of the money from Puerto Rico's

sugar and other minor products found its way back into the countryside. Not all of it, however, for first the merchants took out the cost of goods provided to rural producers, collected their interest on money loaned for the purchase of slaves and equipment, and took for themselves a handsome profit for their services as middlemen in the trading between Puerto Rico and Spain.

In addition to the concentration of military, merchant, and government power in San Juan, two other important elements in Puerto Rican society focused there. The Catholic Church—arbiter and defender of morality and an institution of tremendous importance in the economic, social, and political life of the colony—had its seat in San Juan. There the Cathedral was built; there the Bishop and Inquisitor General (the same person) for all the Indies lived and exercised his office. The Church's tithe—the legal tenth of everything produced in Puerto Rico, assigned to the support of the Church—paid for ecclesiastic expenses in San Juan. Heretics were tried before the Holy Inquisition in San Juan and, when the judgment so required, they were burned there. Church officers charged with that duty examined the crew of every arriving slave ship to make certain that religious heresy was not introduced into the island, and they performed the catechization and baptism of Africans required by law before they could be sold as slaves to work in the countryside. And the Church provided what education was available to the children of upper-class families.

The other important element concentrated in San Juan was the artisan class. Carpenters, tailors, bakers, shoemakers, stonemasons, and candlemakers were encouraged to migrate to Puerto Rico. They settled mostly in San Juan, where they plied their crafts and formed their craft guilds in accordance with Spanish tradition. They, too, were largely dependent on the military/government and merchant classes for their existence. The military and the urban upper classes were the artisan class's most important customers; it was from the merchants that wax, iron, tools, and fabric had to be obtained.

In the countryside, most of the people were involved with sugar; the conditions of sugar production divided people among several categories. At the bottom were those whose labor was required for the cultivation, harvesting, transporting, and milling of sugar cane. They were principally Black slaves whose personal rights and property were most severely restricted. They were supposed to work when, where, and how their masters ordered and in return their bodily needs were to be supplied by their masters. Legally, they had the right to accumulate money and to purchase their freedom; to make that right a reality they were to be given some time each week to work on their own account. They were also understood to have spiritual needs, and it was the duty of both master and the Church to provide religious instruction and to minister to them. A large number of Black slaves were able to obtain their freedom legally, and free

Black people came to make up a large part of Puerto Rico's population. Their intermarriage with whites, Taínos, and *mestizos* (children of white-Indian unions) was common and the racial distinctions that would be made so sharply in future Anglo-American colonies were blurred to a much greater extent in Puerto Rico. Slave rebellions occurred on the plantations, but probably because the plantations were so isolated from each other there was never a major unified uprising of Africans in Puerto Rico. Much more common was the individual flight of slaves who sought freedom in remote parts of the mountains, where they joined small subsistence settlements started by whites and remnants of the Taíno people who had gone into the mountains to escape debt or extreme poverty, or just because they wanted to.

Higher up in the sugar hierarchy than the slave—and sometimes free Black and Taíno—laborers were the sugar masters who at first had been brought primarily from the Canary Islands, where sugar production had already been developed. They were employees of the *ingenios*, or sugar mills, and they understood the process of cooking, stirring, and cooling whereby the juice squeezed from sugar cane could be turned into molasses and sugar. They were at the top of what became a small rural-artisan class on the plantations whose isolation from the city made self-sufficiency necessary. Those of the slave or lowest free classes who had the skills became the plantation mechanics, carpenters, and so forth, and earned a position higher than that of the field laborers.

For a long time after the founding of Puerto Rico as a Spanish colony, all land belonged to the Spanish Crown and was available for use by any colonist. Naturally, the best lands went to those colonists with the most influence, but an important factor in shaping the development of a Puerto Rican people was the fact that almost anyone who wanted to could take up a piece of land and make use of it, at least for his own subsistence. With the growing importance of the sugar industry, it was possible for a number of poor colonists, often *mestizo*, to cultivate sugar cane. But there were other considerations besides land; sugar harvesting required large amounts of heavy hand labor. So, in fact, although land was readily available, a colonist's sugar-cane cultivation was limited by the number of slaves he could afford to buy. An even larger obstacle in the way of the colonist with limited means profiting from the growing market for Puerto Rican sugar was the high cost of building a mill and sugarworks. There were few who could afford to do so, or who could arrange the necessary credit that could make up their lack of ready cash. So there came to be a class of sugar growers who cultivated and harvested the plant and then took it to one of the *ingenios* to be made into sugar. The *ingenio* processed the cane from its own fields first, and the owner took a share of the sugar made from cane that was not his own. This class of sugar-cane growers, dependent on the *ingenio* for transforming their sugar cane into exportable form, came to be called *colonos:* a name that revealed their basic dependence in spite of their apparent independence as landholders and, usually, slaveowners.

At the top of the sugar hierarchy were the owners of *ingenios*. It was they who formed the rural aristocracy of Puerto Rico. Though rural, they usually had connections in San Juan and Spain. It was they who received most of the sugar money that escaped the merchants' and the tax collectors' grasp and who sought to create in Puerto Rico a semblance of Spain's feudalism, ruling over their large estates and their dependents, both slave and free, with little interference from the government. When they traveled it was often in litters carried by slaves, though the litter might not be more of an equipage than a Taíno hammock slung on a pole. The point was made just the same: the rural aristocrat was a man who did not have to dirty his feet on common ground or support his own weight. It was this class, too, from which developed the Puerto Rican *criollo* upper class. *Criollos* were persons born in Puerto Rico of Spanish blood, and the name distinguished them from those Spaniards who came directly from the mother country. *Criollos* identified themselves with Spain, sending their children there to be educated if they could afford it, seeking news of Spain from those who came to the island from the mother country, and following as much as possible the developments of Spanish customs and culture. In time, however, *criollo* identification of themselves as Puerto Rican was to increase until many would feel that they were Puerto Rican first and Spanish second. Eventually, many would identify themselves as Puerto Ricans only. But in the mid and late 1500s that identification was a long way in the future.

As in San Juan the crafts developed in the wake of military fortification, so in rural Puerto Rico a variety of productive enterprises developed in the wake of the sugar industry. Cultivation of local foodstuffs and pigs and cattle developed in order to feed the growing labor force. Horse-raising was stimulated by the need of sugar mills and plantations for draft animals. Livestock, both beef and horses, were also continually in some demand to meet the needs of Spanish fleets and transient troops who called at San Juan on their way to mainland colonies. The importance of cattle continued later as a market for hides developed in Spain, and they were also important in the contraband trade with buccaneers.

Contraband itself became one of Puerto Rico's most important businesses. For one thing, trade with neighboring colonies was prohibited—especially with those established in the Caribbean by France, England, and Holland in defiance of Spanish exclusivism. But direct trade among the islands was more economical than the arduous and heavily taxed trade with Spain. So direct trade was carried on by contraband. Then, too, Spain's monopolist trade system sometimes refused to allow certain goods to be exported legally from Puerto Rico. Traders from European nations other than Spain did not scruple to appear in Puerto Rican waters loaded with goods that Puerto Ricans needed and for which the traders would accept goods that Spain's merchant monopolies would not. So contraband flourished. Usually, Puerto Rico's governors would tacitly recognize the importance of contraband trade in the island's economy and would be careful to take little notice; often, the governors would turn it to their personal account and make up through contraband trade for the slim pickings that their legal transactions offered during most of Puerto Rico's time under Spanish rule.

As the 1500s progressed and the relative prosperity brought by the sugar industry increased, so did attacks by pirates and adventurers of other European powers. As already noted, French attacks were frequent until 1576. Then, toward the end of the century, the rivalry between Spain and England erupted into open war. Englishmen such as Sir John Hawkins and Sir Francis Drake earned fame that has lasted until today for their successes in American waters, where they raided Spanish shipping and sacked and burned Spanish colonial towns. In 1595 Sir Francis Drake was at the height of his fame; he had sailed around the world twice, had filled the coffers of Queen Elizabeth of England with Spanish gold, and had destroyed enough Spanish cities to gain his countrymen's undying gratitude. In that year, the English learned that a Spanish treasure ship had taken refuge in San Juan. Two million pesos in gold were aboard; England sent a fleet commanded by Sir Francis Drake to take it.

On November 22, 1595, the English fleet appeared in San Juan harbor. Under Drake's command were 26 ships; aboard them were 1,500 sailors and 3,000 troops. Behind the walls of San Juan's partially finished fortifications were 1,300 Spanish and *criollo* men and 70 cannon. On the first day, Puerto Rico's guns were able to keep the British fleet at bay; two nights later, in hand-to-hand struggle, Puerto Rico's defenders repulsed an attack by 1,500 Englishmen who got inside the bay in 30 small boats. A Spanish ship was burned in that night's fight, but the English lost 9 boats and more than 400 soldiers. On November 25, the English seemed ready to launch a flank attack by land, but their boats for some reason returned to the fleet and the next day Sir Francis Drake and his force sailed away, leaving Puerto Rico victorious.

Three years later, in 1598, England launched another attack against San Juan, and this time its defenders were not so successful. Though Spain had increased its expenditures for Puerto Rico's defense immediately after Drake's attack, not long before the attack of 1598 an epidemic had badly weakened San Juan's garrison. So it was in a state of reduced numbers and poor morale that Puerto Rico's defenders faced an attack by a fleet of twenty ships under the command of Count Cumberland. This time the English fleet did not risk a frontal challenge to El Morro's guns; instead they landed farther up the coast and launched a flank attack against the city. In two battles fought on June 15, the English forces managed to outflank the soldiers who had come out from the fortress to defend the city. The Spanish troops were caught between two fires and were forced to withdraw behind their fortifications while the English burned and looted the shops and residences of San Juan. Then, comfortably settled in the city, the English set up siege guns and began a steady bombardment of El Morro and La Fortaleza. For several days the Spanish troops held out but, when a section of El Morro's walls began to crumble under the heavy bombardment, they were finally forced to surrender. It was the last time that the city's defenses would fail until the year 1898 when, obsolete in the face of modern naval gunnery, they failed to halt the invasion of the United States forces.

Even in victory the English were able to keep possession of Puerto Rico for only sixty-seven days. English hopes of turning Puerto Rico into a British colony were abandoned after a severe epidemic of dysentery took the lives of four hundred Englishmen. Count Cumberland and his forces withdrew

in the face of what both English and Spanish saw
as the hand of God raised to defend Puerto Rico.
But the English were not prevented from carrying
off a sizable amount of loot, or from destroying
much of the city before abandoning it. In his *Historia de Puerto Rico*, José Luis Vivas describes the
booty carried off by Cumberland's forces as "one
boatload of Black slaves, another of pearls, tanned
skins, ginger, sugar, eighty cannons and the organ
and bell from the cathedral."[2]

The difficulty and slowness of communications
between Puerto Rico and Spain is illustrated by the
fact that the next year a Spanish fleet arrived with
orders from the king of Spain to drive the English
off the island and to restore the Spanish flag. They
found that the Spanish flag was flying, but beneath
the flag there was desolation.

Going into the seventeenth century, Puerto
Rico, as a Spanish colony, could not be described
as prosperous, nor could she be for some time to
come. Spanish Puerto Rico survived. But the
growth of sugar production that had seemed so
promising for a time had slowed; though sugar
production continued, it no longer could earn for
the island the kind of money needed to bring
prosperity in a world of traders. A few figures il-
lustrate clearly the rise and fall of Puerto Rico's
sugar production in the sixteenth century. In the
year 1535, sugar mills in Puerto Rico produced
10,000 pounds. Then, as a result of the slight direct stimulus provided by Spain, production rose

to 450,000 pounds in 1582. But, by the year 1602, production had fallen to only 25,000 pounds.

These figures represent sugar production, and perhaps they might seem to suggest that Puerto Rico had lost its capacity for growing sugar cane and for making sugar. That is not true. What is true is that Puerto Rico could no longer sell the sugar it could produce, or could not sell it for a price that made its production worthwhile. The *Compañía de las Indias* in Seville, the commercial monopoly controlling trade between Spain and its colonies, restricted the market for sugar. Further, when the Spanish government withdrew its direct economic support of Puerto Rico and, instead, ordered the Viceroyalty of New Spain (Mexico) to make an annual contribution for the military defense of the island, the shortage of capital that was already a problem became more acute. Interest rates on money loaned by the monopoly's merchants rose to a level that made it almost impossible to finance sugar production. In essence, the *Compañía de las Indias* had tightened its hold on the sugar growers until it was the only one that could profit from Puerto Rico's sugar industry.

Puerto Rico's sugar decline is often blamed on improved production methods in other Caribbean islands—particularly those where other European powers had taken over—which put Puerto Rico at a competitive disadvantage. It is true that as other European powers developed their own Caribbean sugar sources the European market became more

competitive. Still, if the *Compañía de las Indias* had
felt that it was losing money because of Puerto
Rican inefficiency in production, it seems more
likely that it would have eased credit in the island
in order to promote modernization, rather than
increase the cost of credit. The fact is, heavy pressures were brought to bear on Puerto Rican sugar
growers to keep them producing sugar even when
they could no longer realize a profit.

Puerto Rico's planters began to abandon sugar
cane in favor of ginger and tobacco; in 1602 the
cultivation of ginger was prohibited by law and
tobacco was banned in 1608. Neither ban was effective. Faced with a choice between growing sugar
and trading legally within a system that reserved
all of the profits to Spanish merchants and their
island agents, or of growing ginger and tobacco
illegally for a contraband trade that at least
brought necessities into the island in return, Puerto Rico's planters ignored the law. Ginger became
the island's principal cash crop. In legal trade with
Spain, hides became the most important export
item and provided some cash income for the rural
people who hunted and skinned wild cattle in the
mountains.

It was among those rural dwellers that now,
in the early seventeenth century, a new Puerto
Rican people was beginning to develop. Scattered
throughout the mountains, living usually in isolated and remote places, people who were either so
poor that they had to accept self-sufficiency or so

independent that they would accept poverty developed a simple subsistence way of life that resembled that of the Taínos more than the Spanish. Their houses were thatched like the Taíno *bohíos;* they cultivated Taíno crops, slept in hammocks, learned the medicinal and magical uses of herbs. In the cities, Spaniards and upper-class *criollos* called them *jíbaros*, the name of a South American Indian people. Originally, the term was not applied out of high respect, but it has come to stand for Puerto Rico's rural people and so for the mass of Puerto Rico's people. European blood, African blood, Indian blood mixed in almost endless combinations to create the *jíbaro*. The Catholic faith was modified by the Indian and African beliefs which are too often labeled primitive superstitions. Isolated almost completely from the culture, ideas, and technologies developing in Spain, the *jíbaros* developed ways of their own—and at the same time preserved some things, such as certain pronunciations of the Spanish language, that time and progress eliminated from the mainstream of Spanish culture.

Urban as well as rural life had continued its slow development in Puerto Rico, creating focal points for commerce and for the legitimate links with the outside world. Coamo, Arecibo, San Germán, and San Juan were the four towns on the island. Legal trade was restricted to the port of San Juan; contraband trade went on everywhere. In San Juan the business of cleaning up the mess left by the

English and of renewing and enlarging fortifications went on. Pirate attacks on shipping and isolated coastal settlements continued. Slave traders
with licenses from the king of Spain continued to
arrive in San Juan, though there was little money
for the purchase of slaves and, with the big drop in
sugar production, less incentive than before for
buying them. Garrison troops on meager pay and
scanty supplies walked desultory sentry duty along
El Morro's walls and did little else. Though there
was little money and little glamour, life was neither
desperate nor devoid of amusement. Dances were
frequent and so were religious celebrations. Cockfighting and horse races were popular, and the
natural beauty of sea and island was breathtaking.
As for excitement, who needs more than must
accompany an attempted invasion by foreign
forces? Spain's continued struggles with other
European powers insured that Puerto Rico would
have enemies.

In the year 1625, it became Holland's turn to try
to take Puerto Rico. Spain claimed possession of
the Netherlands, and Holland, aided by Spain's
Protestant enemies, was at war with Spain for independence. In order to cripple Spain in America, the Dutch West Indies Company was formed
and it joined the ranks of those eager to tear
pieces from Spain's American possessions. In September 1625 a Dutch fleet of seventeen ships
carrying 2,500 invasion troops appeared at San
Juan.

There was a new governor on the island, Juan de Haro, who made immediate dispositions for San Juan's defense. Anticipating that the Dutch would repeat Cumberland's basic strategy, de Haro posted his troops to prevent a flanking attack on the city. But the Dutch fleet's commander, Balduíno Enrico, chose a different tactic. Taking unwitting advantage of the fact that de Haro's troop dispositions had left the guns of El Morro badly undermanned, Enrico sailed his fleet directly into the bay. De Haro managed to get his soldiers back inside El Morro, and San Juan's inhabitants had time to flee to the countryside, but Enrico and his forces got possession of the city, as Cumberland's soldiers had done before them. This time, however, although El Morro's defenders numbered only three hundred and thirty men, El Morro's walls stood up against the Dutch bombardment and de Haro refused to surrender. Furthermore, after several days of siege the Spanish and *criollo* soldiers began to come out of El Morro and attack the Dutchmen in their own trenches. A *criollo* captain, Juan de Amézquita, earned great credit for his leadership in raids against the Dutch, and his name is among the earliest on the list of *criollo* fighting men who built the reputation of the Puerto Rican soldier.

Dutch bombardment and Spanish counterattacks continued until finally Enrico threatened to burn San Juan if the defenders of El Morro did not surrender. De Haro refused; Enrico's sol-

diers burned the town. Government records were
burned and the library of the Bishop was destroyed. In the midst of the conflagration, Captain
Amézquita led a Spanish attack from El Morro
against the Dutch and at the same time citizens of
San Juan who had fled into the countryside returned armed and organized for battle. They took
the Dutch from the opposite side, catching them
between two fires. The Dutch fled, first to their
ships, then away from the island.

Once again Puerto Rico had survived attack by
superior force, but also once again San Juan would
have to be rebuilt. For Spain, which for long periods seemed to forget that Puerto Rico existed,
each successful defense of the island against European attack meant a staving off of her impending
collapse as master of America.

4
A CENTURY OF SIEGE

In the seventeenth century a new era opened for America and, consequently, for Puerto Rico. Ever since Spain had reached across the Atlantic and locked together forever the two halves of the world, other European powers had made war on her ships and her colonies and had challenged her right to exclusive possession. The European struggle for a balance of power, for religious authority, for temporal exercise and recognition of the Divine Rights of royal houses spilled over into American waters, where Spain's enemy of the moment could deal her crippling blows at relatively little cost.

In the vastness of America a few English, Dutch, or French ships could be anywhere; if she were to protect her colonies, Spain must be everywhere. The strain and the expense of trying to do that greatly weakened Spain's military might in Eu-

rope. Too, Spain depended greatly on American
wealth to finance her European wars, so when a
European enemy could interrupt the flow of gold
it not only meant an immediate profit for the at-
tacker, but also that Spain's power to put soldiers
into the field and ships upon the sea was lessened.
Of course, English kings and French kings needed
money for their armies and navies as much as
Spanish kings did, but whereas Spain relied on
conquest, adventure, and the king's right to a royal share of all his subjects owned to fill his treasury,
other European powers learned to rely on the
burgeoning wealth of their bourgeoisie whose
mercantile revolution was proving that interest
rates, exchange rates, and trading profits could be
mightier than the sword.

By the seventeenth century Spain had lost the
struggle in Europe, though it would be a long and
agonizing time before she could admit it. And
while Spain proudly bled in defense of medieval
ideals, the strongest of the European powers discovered that America held prizes they valued even
more highly than the chance to humble Spain or
to snatch a pirate prize of Mexican silver or Peru-
vian gold. Sugar, coffee, tobacco, fine hardwoods,
dyewoods, spices, molasses, corn, hides, ginger,
furs: all the American things that could enrich
Europe's life could enrich European merchants.
Trade was more profitable than rape, though not
necessarily much more gentle. With Spain's power
to prevent them sadly weakened, France and Hol-

land and England made permanent colonies in America to provide them with bases for trade.

For a time, the trade rivalry among these European powers eased their direct military pressure against Spanish possessions, though it certainly did not end aggression. France, England, and Holland all acquired Caribbean colonies. Even Denmark gained control of what are now the U.S. Virgin Islands. To the north, on the American mainland, English joint-stock companies established colonies. Holland set up shop on the tip of Manhattan Island in the great natural harbor at the mouth of the Hudson River, considering it an excellent base from which to raid the Caribbean. In the Spanish colonies, Spain continued to command, but her actual rule was weakened, her support decreased, and the colonists were more and more thrown upon their own resources.

In Puerto Rico the effects of Spain's decadence were particularly evident. Trade with the mother country decreased to such an extent that years sometimes passed without the arrival of a Spanish ship. The only real income for the island was the *situado*, the yearly contribution made by Mexico, and that was intercepted by pirates so often that in one period of five consecutive years the money failed to arrive. Contraband trade was carried on either by barter or through merchants wealthy and influential enough to be exempt from the governor's suspicion. In neither case did contraband trade provide the island's government, or the municipal *cabildos*, with tax revenue that could support public services, nor was there any way to regulate the distribution of wealth in the island — though the fact is that there was precious little wealth to distribute.

Practically abandoned by Spain, who yet depended on a Spanish Puerto Rico for its weakening hold on American Empire, the island's *criollos* took the initiative of defense on themselves. In San Juan the damage caused by the Dutch was repaired and the fortifications strengthened. A wall was built to enclose the city in an attempt to prevent a repetition of English and Dutch destruction. Vacancies in the Spanish garrison were filled by *criollos* in spite of Spain's military rules that said Spain's soldiers must be Spanish-born. Throughout the island, *criollos* formed militia units, often including free Black men in their ranks. In the face of mounting pressure from pirates and from encroaching French and English occupation of small islands off Puerto Rico's coasts, expeditions sailed from Puerto Rico and carried the island's defense to their attackers' doors. For example, in 1635, 1637, and 1641, Puerto Rican forces drove encroaching Frenchmen from Santa Cruz. In 1673 a French force of seven hundred men attacked the Puerto Rican town of Aguada and were defeated by Black and *criollo* militia. Over and over, from the seventeenth century onward, Puerto Ricans proved themselves willing to defend Puerto Rico, and capable of it. Inevitably, as time passed, they found themselves motivated to do so from a feeling that Puerto Rico was their home, their land, rather than because they owed a duty to a Spanish king to protect an island that was his possession.

Toward the end of the seventeenth century Puerto Rico began its first contacts with the Anglo-Saxons of North America, ancestors of those who would create the United States of America and forefathers of the men who would one day take Puerto Rico from Spain as a prize of war. New Amsterdam passed from Dutch hands into English ones and became New York, but its role as a pirate haven was not changed by that. In the late 1600s pirates from New York raided Spanish coasts and shipping, accounting for a significant portion of those attacks usually labeled simply as English. A little later, moving into the eighteenth century, Philadelphia became a major port for contraband trade (principally exporting wheat flour) with the Caribbean, including Puerto Rico, while Rhode Island became a principal trader in African lives.

Before leaving the seventeenth century, however, some interesting items of the Puerto Rican story are worth noting. In all the sad history of human slavery, the struggle of slaves to flee to some place where they would be beyond their master's reach is a common thread. In Puerto Rico, as has been noted, Black slaves took to the mountains to escape from Spanish and *criollo* slaveowners. But in 1664 four Black slaves who had escaped from the island of Santa Cruz landed on Puerto Rico's

coast. Though slavery was very much a part of the
Puerto Rican social and economic structure, and
repeated codes of conduct and regulations for
Black slaves attest to Puerto Ricans' concern with
keeping Black slaves in subjection, Governor Juan
Pérez de Guzmán offered asylum to these particular refugees. They were given their freedom and it
was declared that from that time forward any
slaves escaped from other islands would be accepted as free persons in Puerto Rico on the sole conditions that they profess the Catholic faith and
swear allegiance to the Spanish king. So many
Black people took advantage of the freedom offered them in Puerto Rico that in 1714 they established their own town, San Mateo do Cangrejos, on
the outskirts of San Juan. Ironically, this took
place in "despotic" Puerto Rico just one year after
"libertarian" England had forced Spain to give
England the exclusive and free right to import and
sell Africans in the Spanish-American colonies.

In the seventeenth century, too, the first important Puerto Rican writers appear. Diego de Torres
Vargas (*Descripción de la Isla y Ciudad de Puerto Rico*)
and Juan Troche y Ponce de León (*Memoria des-
criptiva de Puerto Rico*) made important contributions in the genre of historical chronicles, and
Francisco de Ayerra y Santa María became known
as the first Puerto Rican-born poet of note.

The eighteenth century began with Spain once
again involved in a European war that would have
repercussions in her American possessions. The

War of the Spanish Succession involved England,
France, Spain, and Austria in a contest to resolve
conflicting French and Austrian claims to the
Spanish throne. In Puerto Rico, English ships attacked Arecibo in the year 1702; they were routed
by the militia, largely *criollo*. That same year, a
joint English and French assault on the town of
Loiza was launched from the nearby island of St.
Thomas only to be defeated by Puerto Ricans. The
next year, Dutch soldiers failed in an attack on San
Germán.

Attacks against Puerto Rican and Spanish shipping were nothing new in the island's experience,
but this time another element was added. Puerto
Rican ships, often manned by free Black sailors,
obtained commissions as privateers and struck
back at English shipping. The line between a pri-
vateer and a pirate was always a thin one; as with
privateers of all nationalities, Puerto Ricans often
as not crossed the wrong side of that line and
avenged themselves on whatever ship was handy
for the long, long years that their island had suffered from pirate attacks. Nor did shipping of the
North American colonies escape. In 1717 the colonists of Virginia were complaining that Puerto
Rican pirates had captured an English ship. In
1718 the governor of New York received a complaint that a ship, carrying a cargo owned by the
mayor of the city, had been captured by pirates
from San Juan. In 1730 England protested formal-
ly to the Spanish Court against the lawless acts of

Puerto Rican pirates. Now that the shoe was on the other foot, English governors, diplomats, and merchants condemned the breach of peace at sea and demanded reparations from Spain.

At the same time that England and its colonies were complaining righteously to Spain about the damages they were suffering, they continued to violate Spanish trading laws themselves. England, as has been mentioned, obtained from Spain the right to sell Black people in the Spanish colonies, and under the guise of that agreement greatly increased its contraband trade in Spanish colonial ports. England's North American colonies, meanwhile, had discovered that much profit could be made in illegal trade that carried rum to Africa, Africans to the Caribbean, and molasses from the islands back to New England where it was distilled as rum to be traded in Africa. English merchant companies resented their own colonies' competition; the colonies resented English trade restrictions. Both continued to ignore Spanish laws, to demand Spanish respect for their own, and to deal as best they could with attacks by Puerto Rico's sailors who were tired of having other people tell them what they could and could not do.

It is worth noting, too, that although North American trade with Spanish colonies was both illegal and carried on by private commercial enterprise, colonial governments in North America did not scruple to involve themselves. Arturo Morales Carrión, in his *Origenes de Las Relaciónes Entre Los*

Estados Unidos y Puerto Rico describes how Lieutenant Governor Cadwallader Colden of New York used to write to various governors of the Spanish Empire to recommend the agents of private commercial houses, to request official intervention in the collection of debts claimed by North American merchants, and to request the release of North American ships and sailors captured by Spanish authorities while engaged in illegal trading. But though New York governors and Rhode Island slave traders might recognize the cash value of trade with Spanish America, popular sentiment in the North American colonies preserved the Protestant, Anglo-Saxon fear and contempt of everything Spanish and Catholic that the centuries of English-Spanish conflict had produced. Anglo-Saxon prejudice was increased by the relative ease with which Spaniards in America had mingled with Indians and Africans.

Though Spaniards in Puerto Rico, as well as in other parts of America, were brutal in their conquest of Indians and imposed slavery on Black people, Spanish prejudice was not as extreme as that of Anglo-Saxons. Under Spanish rule, freedom from slavery was significantly easier to obtain than it was for Blacks in the Anglo-American colonies, and Black freedmen and free women enjoyed greater rights and liberties in Spanish colonies than in those of England. One evidence of this is that a sizable proportion of Black people in Puerto Rico were free. In some of the southern Anglo-

American colonies, by contrast, it was against the
law to set a Black slave free unless his transportation out of the colony was guaranteed at the same
time. Also, intermarriage between Spaniards and
Indians or Black people was tolerated to a much
greater extent in the Spanish colonies than in the
Anglo-American ones. Anglo-American reaction
to the "mixed blood" common in Puerto Rico, for
example, fused the Anglo contempt held for both
the Spanish nation and for nonwhite peoples.

A Rhode Island sailor named John George, captured by Puerto Rican pirates in 1748 and held
prisoner in San Juan for two months, wrote of his
adventures and gave his impressions of Puerto
Rico and its people. He thought the island was
magnificent, but described its inhabitants as "mere
devils." He was particularly disgusted by the way
Puerto Rico provided a sanctuary for Black slaves
escaped from English, Danish, and Dutch colonies,
often arriving with fine ships stolen from their
masters. In the New York colony, not many years
before, the rumor of a Black uprising seemed to
couple itself automatically with fear of a Spanish
Catholic invasion and produced the kind of hyster-
ical terror that fear of the devil had produced in
Salem. It cannot have eased the fears of Anglo-
Saxons whose fortunes were built on the trade in
African lives to find that free Black men often
played conspicuous roles in Puerto Rican expeditions against English intruders in their neighboring islands, and formed a substantial part of the

crews of Puerto Rican ships that challenged the freedom of English and North American ships to go where they pleased in Spanish waters.

The beginnings of relations between Puerto Rico and the Anglo-American colonies took place during—and partly in reaction to—a long period of Spanish neglect of the island that had begun in the first part of the seventeenth century. Spain's interest in Puerto Rico began to revive, however, toward the end of the eighteenth century. New attitudes were gaining ground in Spain, and the fact of European penetration in America began to be viewed more realistically. Efforts were made to reform the colonial system and to try to make Spain competitive in trade. Some reforms were beneficial; others created new problems. Attempts to reorganize Puerto Rican landholding created much confusion—partly owing to the loss of documents destroyed when the Dutch burned San Juan in 1625—and ended with public lands virtually eliminated. Another reform that was a mixed blessing put an end to England's importation of slaves. On the one hand, this cut down on England's contraband trade with the island; on the other hand, to deal with the continuing demand for Black slaves in her American possessions Spain decided to make Puerto Rico a port of entry for slaves brought from Africa and a center of distribution for the rest of the Caribbean.

More beneficial to Puerto Rico was Spain's decision to improve the legal trade between the island

and the mother country, to which end the *Compañía de Barcelona* was permitted to trade with Puerto Rico and to carry trade between Puerto Rico and Santo Domingo as well. Though the *Compañía de Barcelona* was scarcely less monopolistic in its trade policies than the *Compañía de las Indias* in Seville, the volume of Puerto Rican trade did increase substantially. More money came into the island, more goods were exchanged, and there was a corresponding increase in intellectual and cultural contact with the world beyond Puerto Rico. Isolation was further decreased by a regular mail service.

In the early 1750s coffee trees were introduced into Puerto Rico from Santo Domingo. In the Cordillera Central the trees thrived and produced well; soon coffee was an important new crop in the economy. The increased earnings from trade, and the regular receipt of the *situado* from Mexico, accelerated economic development in the island and its population began to rise significantly.

The year 1765 brought Field Marshal Alejandro O'Reilly to Puerto Rico with instructions from the Spanish king to study conditions on the island and to recommend reforms. The field marshal was thorough. He ordered a census taken, studied the realities of trade and contraband, investigated living conditions, and reviewed the defenses. The census showed 39,846 colonists and 5,037 Black slaves. Living conditions among the *jíbaros* had changed little in more than a hundred years. Contraband was still carried on everywhere, with Danes trading for food supplies and coffee, English traders concentrating on dyewoods, the Dutch taking tobacco, and everyone trading for cattle. As for the island's defenses, the field marshal found them in sad shape, but began the work of reorganizing the militias and restoring discipline and drill among the garrison troops. Following his recommendations, further work was done on San Juan's defenses to make it one of the most heavily fortified cities in the Caribbean. And just in time, for war with England was once more just around the corner.

This time, Spain declared war on England in the year 1779, joining with France in support of the thirteen colonies that had declared themselves independent of England in 1776. France and Spain occupied England's attention in Europe, as well as providing direct aid to the American colonies. French contributions to the struggle from which the United States of America were born are fairly well known and acknowledged; Spain's assistance is more generally overlooked. Spain provided military assistance in the Florida campaigns against English forces; she made loans to supply the embattled Continental Army; she opened her ports to Continental ships seeking refuge from England's navy. Even before Spain actually declared war against England, ships from the rebelling English colonies sought—and found—safety from the British in Puerto Rican ports. On August

1, 1777, two privateers, the *Endawock* and the *Henry* sailed into the harbor of Mayagüez with a British frigate hot on their heels. The British warship *Glasgow* refused to respect the sanctuary of Puerto Rican waters and demanded the surrender of the two smaller ships. Direct response came from the citizens of Mayagüez, who dragged *Endawock* and *Henry* onto the beach, got their sailors onto dry land, and then ran up the Spanish flag on both ships.

Glasgow's commanding officer sent ashore to protest the Puerto Ricans' behavior, but the local Puerto Rican commander refused to give up either the two ships or their crews. In fact, he suggested to the British commander that he should leave the Puerto Rican port at once. *Glasgow* left.

As had so often happened in the past, Spain's war with England cut drastically into her ability to communicate with her Caribbean colonies. The Mexican *situado* was interrupted once more, and Puerto Rico's trade with Spain fell off sharply. Now, however, Spain recognized this as a problem for Puerto Rico and permitted her to trade with foreign ports, among which those of the new United States became the most important. When peace was once again achieved between England and Spain, freedom of trade with the United States was again revoked. For United States merchants, that meant that they had no legal access to trade in the Antilles, since in the wake of the revolution England had closed her Caribbean ports to them.

Trade with the Caribbean was very important to the United States and with independence a long history began of pressure to obtain access to, or possession of, Spanish colonies. Of particular interest to the United States were Florida, Cuba, and Louisiana. Although the difference in size and proximity to the United States concentrated United States commercial and diplomatic interest in Cuba more than Puerto Rico, it is interesting to note that twenty-nine United States ships entered San Juan legally in the brief period between 1796 and 1801 — a period when war with England once more prompted Spain to permit the island to trade with neutral ports.

During that war, which Spain got into in order to support French royalist attempts to restore monarchy after the French Revolution, San Juan once again faced assault by a major English force. Fresh from their conquest of Trinidad, the combined sea and land forces of Admiral Sir Henry Harvey and General Sir Ralph Abercromby appeared off the Puerto Rican coast on April 17, 1797. Apparently intending to follow the basic strategy of Cumberland's success in 1598 seven thousand English troops landed a few miles to the east of San Juan and, while the fleet blockaded San Juan's port, the troops began their march to the city. Spanish troops harassed them, but could not prevent their reaching the bridge of San Antonio that linked San Juan to the mainland. There, however, the English advance was stopped. For two weeks, General Abercromby's soldiers tried to force an entrance to San Juan while continually forced to repel guerrilla attacks on their rear and flanks mounted by Puerto Rico's *jíbaros* and militias. Frustrated, Abercromby reembarked his troops and withdrew, having accomplished little more than the destruction of a couple of sugar mills that were in the neighborhood. General Abercromby and his seven thousand veteran soldiers had been defeated overwhelmingly by a force of 938 regular soldiers, both Spanish and *criollo;* 2,442 militia, *criollo*, and free Black; and about 1,000 civilians who took up arms to defend their island.

England never attacked San Juan again, but she did not give up her attempts to conquer Puerto Rico. In December 1797 the militia and citizens of Aguadilla repulsed an English assault; in 1799 the English tried again at Cabo Rojo, and were again defeated. Two attempts to land at Ponce, in 1800 and 1801, failed in the face of Puerto Rican resistance and, also in 1801, a second try at Aguadilla completed the list of English defeats at the hands of Puerto Ricans. The war between Spain and England ended with the Treaty of Amiens in 1802 and English attacks on Puerto Rico ceased.

The last half of the eighteenth century had been a time of great change for all America. For Puerto Rico, the rhythms of life and growth of nearly two hundred and fifty years had been broken. Eighteen new towns were founded, bringing the total to thirty-four by the end of the century.

Puerto Rico's population had grown through the centuries to about 44,000 as estimated by O'Reilly in 1765, then increased to more than 100,000 by 1787. In that year, the population was made up of 79 percent free white or mixed racial ancestry; 11 percent Black or mulatto slave; 8 percent free Black; and 2 percent Indian. The island economy had expanded considerably through more diversified production and wider trade. Sugar had begun a recovery, based on a system of large plantations and with its principal market in the United States. Tobacco and coffee provided cash crops for smaller farmers, who also cultivated the local food crops. In the last years of the century Spain's war with England interrupted trade to some extent, but it also freed Puerto Rico to trade with other nations. The loss of the *situado* from Mexico during those war years, however, seriously handicapped the island government's ability to carry out any public projects, while the tensions and expenses of facing repeated English attacks on its coasts helped slow the progress of the previous years.

Puerto Rico's increased population and commerce had raised the *criollo* social consciousness while at the same time increasing the numbers of recently arrived Spaniards, in whose hands the power and wealth of the island was still largely concentrated. The Spaniards tended to look down on the *criollos*. *Criollos*, for their part, had gained a sense of their worth during the last half century of

struggle both on sea and on land; they felt Puerto
Rico was theirs because they had been born in it,
because the majority of them lived in contact with
its soil, and because they had done so much to
defend it. From the beginning of the nineteenth
century, until the occupation of the island by the
United States military in 1898, the story of Puerto
Rico would primarily be the story of the *criollo*
demand for recognition of their rights in their
own land, and for that land's recognition by the
world.

5

THE FIGHT FOR
SELF-RULE

THE FIRST MAJOR period of Puerto Rico's history
ended with the eighteenth century. It was the period in which Puerto Rico developed its existence as
a unique entity. The second period began with the
nineteenth century and extends to the present.
Throughout this period Puerto Rico has struggled
to express and define its being; to create the necessary conditions for its cultural, social, economic,
and political fulfillment; and to secure the recognition of its right to be master in its own house. In
the nineteenth century its struggle for the rights of
responsible selfhood found its principal opposition
in Spain; in the twentieth century its struggle
would be with the United States.

The inherent division between Spaniard and
Puerto Rican that was contained in Spain's colonial system became more acute in the nineteenth
century. Culturally, politically, and economically,

Puerto Rico's possibilities were limited by a small ruling class of Spaniards whose authority and interests resided in Spain. At the top of the power structure in Puerto Rico was the governor, who was always a Spaniard, almost always a military man, and whose power on the island was unlimited. He made laws by decree, controlled the executive apparatus that enforced their execution, and sat as supreme judge of those who were charged with violating them. As Royal Vicepatron he had great authority in the administration of the Church. This was a matter of genuine importance to the people of Puerto Rico since the Church was one of the island's fundamental institutions and controlled both public and private education. In his capacity as Intendente, or the head of Treasury affairs, the governor had great power over the economic life of the island. And, just to round things out, he was the commander of all army and navy forces in the island.

In all fairness, it should be said that the pressures on any governor to use his authority to benefit Spaniards rather than Puerto Ricans must have been enormous. A Spaniard himself, his natural circle of friends on the island was composed of other Spaniards doing military or commercial duty there. His own political and military career depended on his relationship with the rich and powerful of Spain—and the wealthy Spanish merchants temporarily living in San Juan were more likely to have the ear of someone rich and powerful in Spain than were the island's *criollos*. Too, the governor's first duty to his king was to preserve Puerto Rico as a Spanish possession, and that included preserving it against any Puerto Ricans who might prefer independence. Cultural, political, economic, and military strengths developed by Puerto Ricans could all be seen as potential threats to Spain's dominance: many governors took that point of view.

For *criollos* of all classes there was no legal avenue to participation in the shaping of decisions that affected their lives. Some were wealthy enough to gain personal entrance to the influential circle of Spaniards who ruled the island, but they could do so only by identifying themselves with that group's values and attitudes. As the historian, Professor Lidio Cruz Monclova, has written, the *criollos* "had no representative at the metropolitan center. They even lacked freedom of movement from town to town, permission being required from municipal authorities until the mid-nineteenth century. They did not participate in the enactment of laws nor did they have a representative organ which could control the governor's excesses."[1] Under such conditions, as the growing Puerto Rican identity became a reality and Puerto Ricans became increasingly aware of their own painting, literature, and music—and gained self-confidence from their military successes—it was inevitable that *criollos* would struggle for the right to have a voice in their own destiny. At first, their ambition was usually expressed as a desire for equality with Spaniards, but before long many began to define their goals and their needs as distinct from those of Spain and to seek a kind of separation that would allow them to make their own decisions.

Two external events at the beginning of the nineteenth century profoundly affected Puerto Rico's struggle for self-realization. The first was the invasion and near-conquest of Spain by Napoleon Bonaparte that shattered the structure of Spanish government and altered the relationship between the mother country and her colonies. The second was the wave of rebellions in Spanish America as colony after colony sought independence from Spain.

News that Napoleon had invaded Spain and had taken King Fernando VII to France as a prisoner, substituting Joseph Bonaparte on the Spanish throne, came to Puerto Rico on July 24, 1808, with the arrival of the Spanish sloop-of-war *Intrepida*. Captains Manuel Francisco Jáuregui and Juan Jabat had more news, too; the Spanish people were in rebellion against the French and their puppet king, and in the various provinces of Spain juntas were being formed to organize the resistance and to reform the legitimate government. Captains Jáuregui and Jabat came as representatives of the Junta of Seville to ask the governor of Puerto Rico to declare his continued loyalty to King Fernando and to ask support from the people of Puerto Rico in the fight to expel the French usurper. The responses of both Governor Toribio Montes and the people of Puerto Rico were overwhelmingly in support of Fernando VII and the Junta of Seville against Bonaparte. Puerto Rico's reaction was typical of that of the other Spanish American colonies, though in a very short time most of the colonies' rebellion against the French usurper would continue as rebellion against Spain.

The Spanish juntas, supported vigorously by the Spanish people, began to enjoy successes in their war against Napoleon. In 1809 the various juntas were replaced by a Supreme Council of Spain and the Indies. In recognition of their support, Spanish American colonies were declared to be integral with the Spanish monarchy and were invited to send representatives to the Supreme Council. For the first time, Puerto Rico's *criollos* were to have a voice in the government that ruled their lives. Governor Montes made the Supreme Council's decree known in the island and gave the municipal governments of San Juan, San Germán, Aguada, Arecibo, and Coamo the responsibility for electing a representative to Spain. The man elected was a *criollo*, Ramón Power Giral, born in San Juan of Spanish parents in 1775. He had studied in Spain and in France and at the time of his election was in Santo Domingo, fighting with the Spanish and Puerto Rican troops who were trying to recover the Spanish portion of that island from the French.

Power's election coincided with the arrival of a new governor in Puerto Rico, Salvador Meléndez Bruna. Governor Meléndez shared the opinion that *criollo* achievements were a potential threat to Spain's possession of the island, but he obeyed the decree of the Supreme Council, honored the Puerto Rican election, and ordered Ramón Power Giral to return at once from Santo Domingo to Puerto Rico. At a public farewell ceremony for Power, celebrated in San Juan's cathedral, Bishop Juan Arizmendi, the first and only Puerto Rican clergyman to rise to the bishopric, exhorted Power to "protect and sustain the rights of our compatriots." That moment, when one distinguished Puerto Rican spoke publicly to another—and in his use of the word "compatriot" plainly meant it to refer to the people of Puerto Rico—is the moment that Lidio Cruz Monclova describes as representing "the awakening consciousness of a Puerto Rican identity, a unique society born of three centuries of a common insular existence."[2] With Power, on his mission to the Cortes of Cadiz, where a constitution for Spain was to be created, went the hopes of those Puerto Ricans who looked to a reform of the Spanish government and its relations with its overseas possessions for a solution to Puerto Rico's problems and improvement of its second-class status.

Meanwhile, the wave of independence in South America was gathering to sweep the continent into rebellion and civil wars that would not end until

Spain had lost its last continental possession. As early as 1806, a Venezuelan patriot had attempted armed rebellion to achieve independence from Spain. A true American international revolutionary, Francisco de Miranda fought against the British during the North American colonies' war for independence, then went to France to take part in the French Revolution. For his early, though abortive, attempt to free Venezuela from Spain, Miranda earned the title, "The Precursor." Later, with Simón Bolívar, Miranda led the first concerted fight against Spain in Venezuela.

In response to the rebellion brewing in Venezuela, which Spain's government feared would spread to Puerto Rico and its other Caribbean possessions, Puerto Rico's governor received—in the same year that Power set off to represent the island in the Cortes—special powers to take any action he might find necessary to suppress Puerto Rican rebellion by those who wanted independence from Spain. However, the liberalizing effects of Spain's new attitudes toward the island made it difficult for revolutionaries to recruit support, especially since the war begun in Venezuela by Bolívar and Miranda seemed to be going against them. Governor Meléndez had little need to use his special powers, but the fact remains that while Spain held out a carrot with one hand, it had already prepared a stick for the other.

Power took more than his people's hopes with him to Spain; he took written instructions prepared by each of the municipalities that had participated in his election. If there could be any doubt that the Puerto Rican people had an understanding of their problems or were equipped to find their own solutions to them (a doubt later expressed or implied in too many United States reports for the suggestion to be rhetorical), a brief look at the instructions given their representative should go a long way to dispel them. In "The Puerto Rican Political Movement of the 19th Century," prepared for the United States – Puerto Rico Commission on the Status of Puerto Rico, Cruz Monclova has summed up the instructions and recommendations given to Power to guide his efforts on behalf of Puerto Rico.

In order to improve the intellectual environment of the island, Power Giral was requested to emphasize the development of public education and the establishment of a university of humanities and sciences, insofar as the education of youth was seen as the foundation on which the state is built. Public sanitation was also an issue at hand, and the establishment of hospitals and health centers was considered to be essential to the proper functioning of a civilized community. The creation of a school of mechanic arts with rehabilitation facilities for both sexes was suggested as one answer to the problem of juvenile delinquency, since preventive laws tend to be more effective than penal ones. To foster internal communications and thereby overcome another major obstacle to the prosperity of the island, it was recommended that Power request construction of roads and bridges to replace the grossly unsatisfactory conditions for transport. To help raise the moral and material level of workers, Power's instructions included a request for the division and distribution of untilled land belonging to the state, and the foundation of guilds with appropriate rules and statutes. In order to improve the administration of justice, popular election of the lieutenants of war and their seconds, the major sergeants, were to be requested instead of having them appointed by the Governor, as well as the separation of Puerto Rico from the jurisdiction of the Cuban *Audiencia* and its incorporation into that of Venezuela, given its proximity and accessibility.

In the case of agriculture, the principal source of income, it was Power's role to demand the abolition of the tax on forced supply of meats and to repeal the prohibition on the growing of wheat, as well as a reduction of various duties and the free importation of agricultural tools from abroad. On behalf of insular industry, he was to solicit the right to distill and export rum, in addition to a franchise for the island's commerce, freedom of trade with foreign nations for a period of 15 to 20 years, and the establishment of new ports. Freedom to export was seen as a means to protect the cattle industry, and a system of proportional taxation was added to the list as well. Finally, in order to break up the tight circle which kept *criollos* from attaining official positions, Power was to defend the claim that native-born Puerto Ricans be given preference for public posts on the island. The foregoing reflects the impact of various socio-political ideas of liberal theologians and jurists in Spain during the preceding centuries, as well as the influence of the democrat chartists of North America and European reformers—an effective demonstration that the Enlightenment had not bypassed the current of island liberalism.[3]

The municipality of San Germán had an additional instruction for Power: he was to tell the

Cortes that Puerto Rico claimed the right to independence if the Supreme Council should be defeated by Napoleon.

And a few months later, in 1810, another more direct and less polite expression of Puerto Rican readiness to define its own identity was contained in a note that Antonio Cortabarría found nailed to his door. Cortabarría was on a special mission from Spain to do something about the Venezuelan revolution. He had decided to recruit a force of Puerto Rican militia to fight against Miranda and Bolívar, when the note he found made him change his mind. It read: "This people, docile enough to obey the authorities that it recognizes, will never permit one single American to be taken out of the island to fight against his brothers of Caracas."

As the Puerto Rican Bishop Arizmendi's use of the term "compatriot" reflected the growing sense of Puerto Rican identity, so the use of the term "American" in the rebellious note nailed to Cortabarría's door points up the schism between Spain and Puerto Rico and expresses a sense of identity with other people of the Caribbean geographic system of which it is a part.

In Cádiz, Ramón Power Giral was elected vice-president of the Cortes which set to work to write a Spanish National Constitution. The first of its kind to be approved in Spain, the constitution became Supreme Law in 1812 and in the same year was proclaimed in Puerto Rico. The parts relating to Puerto Rico affirmed as fundamental rights many of the island reformists' political aspirations.

Puerto Rico was declared an integral part of the monarchy, reaffirming by constitutional law what had been expressed by Spain's interim government, the Supreme Council. Full Spanish citizenship, however, was limited to free white persons. Such basic civil rights as the inviolability of the home and personal property were guaranteed to Spain's new citizens in Puerto Rico. Their right to representation by voice and vote in the Spanish Cortes—in which the constitution vested the right to legislate for Spain—was guaranteed; Puerto Rico's deputy to the Cortes was to be elected indirectly by vote of all citizens aged twenty-five years and over. In each parish the voters would elect an elector; the electors within each district (*partido*) would then elect a district representative. In San Juan, the district representatives would meet to elect a deputy who would represent Puerto Rico in the national Cortes.

Administratively, though the office of appointed governor was retained under the Constitution of 1812, his powers were substantially broken up. The office of Intendente (head of Treasury) was separated from that of governor, and a Provincial Assembly of nine members was created to provide Puerto Rican participation in the island government. Two seats in the Provincial Assembly automatically went to the governor and the Intendente. The remaining seven were filled electively throughout the island, there being a property requirement for the eligibility of candidates. Duties and responsibilities of the Provincial Assembly, according to Cruz Monclova, were "to establish the basis for proportional taxation, to examine the accounts of the townships and regulate the investment of public funds, to propose public works, to protect the interests of welfare and religious institutions, and to promote agriculture, industry, and commerce, as well as public education."[4]

The separation of powers produced immediate practical benefits in Puerto Rico. In matters of trade and commerce especially, the creation of a separate office of the Treasury headed by an Intendente largely independent of the governor, led to real economic stimulus and to the correction of some abuses of very long standing. The first Intendente appointed under the new laws, Alejandro Ramírez, worked diligently to reorganize the economy, armed with specific recommendations from the Cortes which, in turn, reflected Ramón Power Giral's success in representing his countrymen's point of view.

Alejandro Ramírez was convinced that the island's economic health could truly be achieved only by mobilizing its own resources. Among the changes achieved by Ramírez were the opening of five new ports to trade and the establishment of customs houses in them. Agricultural tools and implements were allowed duty-free entry, while import tariffs on certain foodstuffs and merchandise necessary to the island's everyday life were standardized and greatly reduced. In the process of tariff reorganization, the de facto monopoly on wheat flour which had for so long been a source of extra profit to the island's governors and an especially heavy burden on Puerto Rico's people, was broken.

Puerto Rico's need for wheat flour was a constant, since it was regarded as a necessity in the Puerto Rican diet. The cultivation of wheat, however, was forbidden on the island. A substantial trade in flour had been developed between Anglo-American merchants and the governors of Puerto Rico. Even when foreign trade was prohibited by Spain, the governor could exercise emergency powers to admit ships bearing flour on the basis of shortages in the island. In this trade the governor purchased flour for the island with public funds and strictly controlled its sale to consumers. According to Ramón Power Giral there were very few governors who did not profit substantially from this trade and at the expense of Puerto Ricans. In order to keep prices high, the governor had only to keep the supply scarce. In Philadelphia, center for this trade in the United States, there were always merchants and shipowners willing to collaborate.

Alejandro Ramírez opened Puerto Rico's ports to free trade and reduced the tariff on flour to less than a third. This, and other like measures, cut considerably into the profiteering of the governor and his circle of Spanish merchants, but it made many more necessary goods available to the people of Puerto Rico at prices they could afford and stimulated the production and export of their agricultural goods. A measure of Ramírez's real success is that he *increased* the island government's revenues by nearly 300 percent, and saw to it that they went into the island's treasury, where the new Provincial Assembly had a say in how they would be spent.

The optimism created in the island by the reforms that followed the proclamation of the Constitution of 1812 effectively countered in Puerto Rico the spirit of separatism that was sweeping Spanish America. The hopes of separatists were also lowered by the apparent victory, in 1813, of Spain's army over the rebel forces of Bolívar and Miranda. Puerto Rico's separatist conspirators had been understandably disheartened when Francisco de Miranda was brought to the island as a prisoner and locked in El Morro's dungeon. If Venezuela, incomparably bigger and stronger than Puerto Rico, could not succeed against Spain, then what hope had they? Especially when so many could point to the recent reformations and believe that loyalty to Spain could be just as profitable as independence — and the profits much more secure.

But faith in the security of relations with Spain would soon be rudely shattered. In 1814 Spain drove Napoleon's armies from her territory and Fernando VII was restored to the Spanish throne.

Spanish rejoicing was short-lived, for almost immediately Fernando abrogated the Constitution of 1812 and returned Spain to absolute monarchy. Puerto Rico lost her newfound equality and reverted to colonial status. Her people lost their Spanish citizenship and the governor recovered much of his lost power. Yet, although Puerto Rican political hopes had suffered a severe setback that surely reinforced the beliefs of separatists, the people in general did not react as strongly as might have been expected — probably because the Spanish king almost immediately proclaimed a Royal *Cédula de Gracias* that gave the island even greater economic freedom than it had begun to enjoy under the Constitution of 1812. The *Cédula* also recognized the value of some decentralization in the colony's government, though it definitely allowed for less Puerto Rican participation than under the constitution. But the economic benefits were real, as was the Spanish military presence, and for the most part Puerto Ricans busied themselves with accelerating the rate of material progress that had begun with the arrival of Alejandro Ramírez.

One of the chief objectives of Spain's policy as reflected in the *Cédula de Gracias* was to increase Puerto Rico's population, particularly its segment of white people whose primary loyalty would be to Spain. The loss of Louisiana and of Santo Domingo; the bloody but successful rebellion of Haiti's Black people; the turmoil caused by the independence struggles in Venezuela, Mexico, and Buenos

Aires—all had contributed to a flow of white immigrants who came to Puerto Rico because it seemed the American colony least likely to slip from Spain's grasp. The *Cédula* was deliberately designed to increase that immigration, not only from the disturbed areas of America but from Spain as well. White Catholics from countries friendly to Spain could enter Puerto Rico with all their goods and their slaves; they were declared free from taxation for ten years; they were given free land at the rate of six acres per family member and three acres per slave; they were at liberty to leave Puerto Rico with all of their belongings, including any they might have acquired in Puerto Rico; they were promised Spanish citizenship in return for five years' residence in the island.

The *Cédula* also allowed Puerto Rico to trade freely with Spain, with foreign countries friendly to Spain, and with other Caribbean islands. Agricultural tools manufactured in Spain were allowed into Puerto Rico free of duties, and the restriction of shipbuilding in the island was removed. According to José Luis Vivas's *Historia de Puerto Rico:*

> All aspects of island life saw themselves affected by the immigration: new businesses and commercial houses were established; the construction of houses and buildings was improved; the people began to read more and to have more concern for public instruction, so forgotten during three centuries. An evidence of that is the founding of chairs of geography, commerce, mathematics, theology, and medicine. Nevertheless, it

is necessary to point out that they were established by Puerto Rican concern, for Spain went on believing in the old theory that "an ignorant people is easier to keep docile."[5]

New towns were built. The number of schools increased. In the countryside the number of prosperous farms and plantations grew, and so did the number of landless workers forced by necessity into a dependent relationship with landowners. For as new white colonists arrived and were given free lands, it was often found that *jíbaros* were already living and supporting themselves on them. But the *jíbaros* held no legal titles and so they were forced to move or else to remain as *agregados*, resident workers on land owned by someone else. The *criollo* society, *Sociedad Económica de Amigos del País*, worked to provide privately the education for *criollos* that Spain refused to provide.

More and more sons of Puerto Rican families went to Spain, to France, to the United States to study and came back strongly influenced by the liberal ideas Spain was so anxious to keep out of the island. Puerto Rican separatists went to Mexico and plotted for the liberation of Puerto Rico with agents of Simón Bolívar who, in spite of everything, had refused to be defeated in Venezuela. Puerto Rican *criollos* debated the colonial problems of their island and recognized the stultifying effects of colonialism and of slavery—but more and more often *criollos* found themselves with property and benefits that could be jeopardized by rash action.

Two *criollo* factions defined themselves quite clearly. The goal of one faction was autonomy, or self-government without separate nationhood. The other sought assimilation, or a complete identity with Spain under which it would function as one more province within the Spanish nation. The achievement of both of these goals depended, finally, on Spain's willingness to give Puerto Ricans the respect, equality, and dignity that their growing sense of identity demanded. The separatists, on the other hand, were unwilling to depend on Spain for anything. They wanted freedom from Spain and looked toward Puerto Rico's relationship with a free family of Spanish American republics for its security and growth. These three goals—assimilation, autonomism, and separatism—are still today the three alternative goals recognized in Puerto Rico. Today the need is to resolve the island's relationship with the United States, not Spain, and the three goals are statehood, Commonwealth, and independence.

The events of the first few years of the nineteenth century described so far in this chapter reflect the basic elements of growth, struggle, and dissension that affected Puerto Rico's relations with Spain until they were severed by war at the end of the century.

In 1820 another liberal revolution, known as the Riego Revolt, broke out in Spain, and King Fernando VII was forced to restore the Constitution of 1812. He, and all Spaniards, were forced to swear to uphold the constitution on pain of death.

Once again the constitution was proclaimed in Puerto Rico; once again Puerto Ricans elected a representative to the Spanish Cortes and elected members to the island's restored Provincial Assembly. In Spain, Puerto Rico's representative sought increased reforms for Puerto Rican commerce, education, and social services, and he obtained the separation of the governor's civil and military powers. The first civil governor was Francisco González de Linarea; he shared power in the island with Miguel de la Torre, who arrived to take up his post as military governor fresh from defeat in Venezuela at the hands of Simón Bolívar. The Venezuelan victory was followed by rebellion against Spain in Santo Domingo. These events encouraged Puerto Rico's separatists to attempt a revolt in their own island. An invasion from Venezuela was organized under the leadership of General Luis Guillermo Lafayette Doucoudray Holstein which was to take place simultaneously with a Black uprising in the north of Puerto Rico. The goal of this revolt was the establishment of the independent republic of Boricua and the emancipation of the island's slaves. But the rebellion was discovered by the Spanish authorities, the Black revolt was aborted, and Holstein's fleet was detained in Curaçao. At least one of the conspirators, Pedro Dubois, paid for his convictions with his life when Spanish soldiers executed him at El Morro.

An important event in Puerto Rico's struggle to gain recognition by participation in the Spanish system occurred in 1823 when the Puerto Rican deputy to the Cortes, Dr. José María Quiñones, petitioned Spain for what amounted to an autonomous constitution for Puerto Rico. Supported by the Cuban deputy, Félix Varela, the petition was for a set of laws that would specify the duties of the island's governor and that would give real authority to the Provincial Assembly and the municipal governments. Interestingly, this proposal was approved by Spain's Overseas Commission and then by the Cortes itself. It never received final proclamation as law, however, for once again Spanish reactionary forces launched a counterrevolution that once again abolished the constitution and restored to Fernando VII the powers of absolute monarchy. In Puerto Rico, the military governor, Miguel de la Torre, deposed the civil governor and assumed personally all the powers of island government. Once more Puerto Rico reverted to second-class, colonial status.

And so it went. In 1834, during a brief liberal thaw in Spain, Puerto Rico was allowed to send two delegates to the newly formed representative body called *Procuradores*. General de la Torre's arbitrary control of the electoral law angered Puerto Rican liberals, but they elected José Saint Just and Esteban de Ayala and sent them to Spain with instructions to request government reform for Puerto Rico that would guarantee individual and property rights (abused by the absolute powers of Governor General de la Torre), free trade, tax reforms, expansion of agriculture and industry, and more public education. They also were to ask specifically for the restoration of the Provincial Assembly and elected municipal governments. Saint Just and de Ayala returned to Puerto Rico, their petitions having been ignored in Spain. Following that disappointment a number of Puerto Ricans joined with the Spanish Captain Loizaga in a plot to restore the Constitution of 1812 in Puerto Rico. The plot was discovered, Captain Loizaga was exiled, and a number of Puerto Ricans were punished.

Restoration of the Constitution of 1812 was again forced in Spain, however, in 1836. Yet again, Puerto Rican hopes rose and a representative to the Cortes was elected. This time disappointment came even more swiftly, for the next year the Cortes decided—contrary to the constitution—that Cuba and Puerto Rico should be ruled by a special set of laws. Puerto Rico's representative, Juan Bautista Becerra, was refused his seat in the Cortes, as was Cuba's representative.

It was a bitter blow for Puerto Ricans who had struggled in the belief that attainment of their rights was compatible with loyalty to Spain. Now they saw the Constitution of 1812, which a Puerto Rican had helped to write, made the law of Spain but with themselves excluded from its benefits. The Cortes was for Spain; a military governor possessed of absolute powers was for Puerto Rico.

In 1838 another rebellion plot was under way on the island, led by Puerto Ricans among whom were Andrés Vizcarrondo Martínez, Buenaventura Quiñones, and Juan Quiñones. Their plan involved the mutiny of the Granada Regiment and their object was to declare Puerto Rico independent of Spain. This conspiracy was discovered as the ones before it had been, and the island's new governor, Marshal Miguel López de Baños, took violent action against the conspirators. Some were killed; others were exiled. Buenaventura Quiñones was imprisoned in El Morro, where one day he was found hanged in his cell.

From the governorship of de la Torre through that of José María Marchessi—a period of forty-two years—Puerto Rico was governed by eleven lieutenant generals and three field marshals. All were possessed of "all the breadth and reach of powers that sovereignty can attribute," as the special authorization extended to Governor Meléndez in 1810 had expressed it. Among the powers were those of dismissing any government employee for any reason that seemed sufficient to the governor; of arresting and holding any person on the island without consideration of condition or privilege, and of sending them wherever the governor thought best; of preventing the entry of any person from Venezuela who failed to satisfy the governor as to his loyalty; and of carrying out whatever act might appear necessary for the peace of the island. During those forty-two years the following are only a few of the things governors found indispensable to Puerto Rico's peace.

GOVERNOR MIGUEL DE LA TORRE: A 10 P.M. curfew in the towns, and a ban on reunions after dark. Later on de la Torre decided the people would be less troublesome if they were more festive. So, for the good of the island, he encouraged dice games, card rooms, dances, cockfights, and horse races.

GOVERNOR LÓPEZ DE BAÑOS: A decree that punished anyone found to be without work or income.

GOVERNOR SANTIAGO MÉNDEZ VIGO: A decree forbidding mustaches or goatees; the prohibition of visits to Puerto Rico by foreigners; a decree requiring all Black people to stay in their houses after 11 P.M.

GOVERNOR JUAN PRIM, COUNT OF REUS: The shooting of a bandit known as El Aguila who had stolen the governor's horse and the subsequent total ignoring of the island's highest court which found the shooting to have been a murder; a special decree of harsh punishments for the suppression of Black people, both slave and free; a prohibition of the movement of ships without the governor's personal permission.

GOVERNOR JUAN DE LA PEZUELA Y CEBALLOS: The prohibition of horse racing; a decree forbidding collective petitions; a decree that classified every person older than sixteen who was not a property owner as a laborer and that required all laborers to carry a passbook in which their employer was to record their place of work, salary, conduct, and date of termination. Pezuela also issued decrees forbidding people to change their residence, rent houses, travel throughout the island, or give parties without prior permission. Pezuela did, on the other hand, repeal Governor Prim's harsh decrees against Black people, and he established a token price for the freeing of newborn slaves at the baptismal font.

The list of government abuses above is but a sample, presented here to show the arbitrariness of life for Puerto Ricans without government of their own. These were not, perhaps, the worst of the abuses committed against Puerto Rico's people, nor were the governors mentioned the worst that Puerto Rico was to know.

But there were other men in Puerto Rico during those years. There was the Spanish priest, Father Rufo Manuél Fernandez, who helped Puerto Rican youth get scholarships to study in Spain. Among those so helped were José Julián Acosta and Román Baldorioty de Castro, both of whom were to figure prominently in Puerto Rican history. There was Rafael Cordero, a Black shoemaker who, besides supporting himself at his trade, ran and taught in a free school for Black children and for children of poor white families. He began this work when he was twenty years old and kept it up until he died at the age of seventy-eight. José Luis Vivas said of Rafael Cordero that he was "the Puerto Rican who in our history comes closest to the concept of a holy man."[6] There was Ramón Betances, a Puerto Rican doctor educated in Paris, who attended the people of Puerto Rico's poorest classes during the terrible cholera epidemic of 1855—an epidemic that took thirty thousand lives. When Governor Pezuela reduced the emancipation price for Black babies at the baptismal font, Betances bought and freed so many Black babies that in 1860 he was exiled from the island. There was Julian Blanco Sosa, self-educated and known as the best office boy in San Juan, who was also exiled in 1860 for having sent a petition to Spain asking for the special laws the Cortes had promised in 1837 when they refused Puerto Rico's representatives their seats.

By 1862 another rebellion against Spain was being planned in Puerto Rico. Headed by Dr. Ramón Betances, Puerto Rican separatists worked to arouse and unite the Puerto Rican people for a revolution that would set the island free. Governor Félix María de Messina warned Betances about his activities, then threatened to hang him. Betance's reply is famous among patriotic Puerto Ricans. "Then know well, General Messina, that the night of that day I will sleep more peacefully than your excellency."[7] He was exiled again, and from St. Thomas proclaimed the Ten Commandments of free men: abolition of slavery; the right to vote on all taxation; freedom of worship; freedom of speech; freedom of the press; free commerce; the right to congregate; the right to own arms; the citizen's inviolability; and the right to elect authority.

In the year of Betances's second exile, 1867, the Spanish Cortes finally asked for delegates from Cuba and Puerto Rico to help determine what the special laws for the Antillean possessions should be. José Julián Acosta, Segundo Ruíz Belvis, and Francisco Mariano Quiñones upset the Spanish government and their own island's conservative elements by ignoring Spain's prohibition on discussion of the slavery issue. Slavery must be ended, they said, with compensation for slaveholders, or without compensation. Spain ignored their demand for abolition as it ignored their other demands for Puerto Rico. And they soon had a chance to learn just how upset the circle of ruling conservatives back in their island was. Ramón Betances (back from exile), Julián Blanco Sosa, Segundo Ruíz Belvis, and a number of others were expelled from Puerto Rico by the governor and ordered to report to the government in Spain. Betances and Ruíz Belvis went instead to New York, where they joined a revolutionary group that was organizing revolution for Cuba and Puerto Rico.

In 1868 the revolutionary organization in Puerto Rico was well advanced, with local groups in a number of places in the island. From New York, Betances bought rifles, a few cannon, and a ship. He appealed to Puerto Rico's liberal leaders—

such men as Román Baldorioty de Castro and José Julián Acosta: men who wrote and spoke fearlessly for Puerto Rico's rights—to join the liberation movement. They declined, preferring to rely on peaceful and legal means to obtain their rights. The only trouble was that Spain and Puerto Rico's governors could change the meaning of "legal" from moment to moment. Betances and his co-revolutionaries went ahead with their planned uprising.

As had happened before, the rebellion was discovered before it was launched. The separatists decided to go ahead anyway and they moved up the date of the rebellion. On September 23, 1868, perhaps a thousand men gathered at a farm outside Lares. The rifles they had counted on were in Santo Domingo; their ship was in St. Thomas. Armed only with machetes and a few odd guns, that night they took the town of Lares. The next day they declared the establishment of the Republic of Puerto Rico, and issued a proclamation calling all Puerto Ricans to arms and promising freedom to any slave who would defend the Republic. Then the liberation army marched on the nearby town of Pepino, where they found troops prepared to receive them. After an unequal battle the rebels were forced to flee. For more than a month the governor's troops hunted them through the mountains until the resistance was broken. Many were killed, many were jailed, and in the aftermath of the revolt many Puerto Ricans who were

liberals but who had refused to take part in the uprising were arrested and imprisoned.

The *Grito de Lares*, as the uprising is known,
failed of its aims. But it still stands as Puerto Rico's
symbol of resistance and today its anniversary,
September 24, is a Puerto Rican holiday.

In Spain the liberal forces within the government were slowly gaining ground: that is, in the
swings back and forth between constitutionalism
and absolutism the constitutionalists were more
and more often in power. When liberal government was on top in Spain, liberal hopes rose in
Puerto Rico. In 1869 Spain had a new constitution;
Puerto Ricans went to the Cortes; suspects and
survivors of the *Grito de Lares* jailed in Puerto Rico
were amnestied.

In 1873 Spain was declared a Republic; after
much pressure from such Puerto Rican representatives as Román Baldorioty de Castro, all slaves in
Puerto Rico were declared free. The Republic did
not last long—only until 1875—but Puerto Rico's
right to be represented before the Spanish government remained more or less intact. On the island,
political parties were formed, divided primarily
between Conservative and Liberal. The Conservatives were the powerful, principally Spanish, class
of merchants, clergy, and government bureaucrats
personally interested in preserving the status quo;
the Liberals represented most of the Puerto Ricans, but not in a solid front. The history of the
party politics of those years is too complex to de-

scribe here, but in general Liberals divided on two issues. The first was whether Puerto Rico's goal should be for full assimilation in Spanish national life, with equality of rights and opportunities with Spaniards of the Peninsula, or whether to seek autonomy. Autonomy meant the recognition that Puerto Rico existed under circumstances different from those of Spain and that the island should be allowed to determine its own policies, while remaining politically and culturally united with Spain. The second issue that divided Liberals — by then autonomists, for the most part — was whether or not to unite the Autonomist party (founded in 1882 by Román Baldorioty de Castro) with one of Spain's national parties in an effort to strengthen its position in the Cortes. One of the strongest proponents of fusion with a Spanish party was Luis Muñoz Rivera, a newspaper editor of strong convictions and a habit of attacking the island government. When the Autonomists refused to agree to fusion, Muñoz Rivera left the party. But, in 1895, when Cuba's second war for independence broke out, Puerto Rico's separatist movement began a strong revival. Many dissident Autonomists who had grown tired of the politicking inside their party began to move into the separatist ranks. Not Muñoz Rivera. Like the earlier liberals who had refused to join Betances, Muñoz Rivera thought revolution would be disastrous for Puerto Rico and he insisted that its goals could be achieved by peaceful means. On his own, he went to Spain, talked to political leaders there, and reached an agreement with Mateo Práxedes Sagasta. Sagasta was leader of the Liberal Monarchist party; he promised Muñoz Rivera that if he became prime minister he would see that Puerto Rico became autonomous. With that victory in his pocket, Muñoz Rivera returned to the island and rallied the Autonomists. In view of Sagasta's promise, most party members agreed to affiliate with the Spanish party.

In 1897 Mateo Práxedes Sagasta became prime minister of Spain. Spain was losing the war in Cuba; the United States press was whipping up popular sentiment for a war with Spain, alleging concern over Spain's treatment of its colonies; and Sagasta had made a promise to Muñoz Rivera. These considerations combined to encourage Spain to go beyond the reforms it was already instituting in order to reduce the anti-Spanish sentiment in America and grant Puerto Rico a charter of autonomy. The charter amounted to a Puerto Rican constitution and provided for genuine self-government, though the island would continue to have a governor appointed from Spain. But his duties were specified and his powers limited. After four hundred years, Puerto Rico was recognized as a separate and self-governing entity with its rights established by a royal decree which plainly stated: "After its approval by the Cortes of the Kingdom, the present Constitution for the Islands of Cuba and Puerto Rico cannot be modified except by virtue of law and by petition of the Island Parliament."[8]

6
THE UNITED STATES OCCUPATION

IN EARLY FEBRUARY 1898, Puerto Rico's autonomous government was inaugurated by a new governor, General Manuél Macias Casado, and the people of Puerto Rico prepared to elect their first Insular Assembly where, for the first time, their own representatives would control the laws under which Puerto Ricans lived. After a century-long struggle, Puerto Ricans' existence as a people had been recognized and their right to govern themselves had been established.

The Autonomous Charter of 1897 provided for a Puerto Rican government in which there was a basic division of powers among the executive, legislative, and judicial branches. The chief executive was a governor general appointed by the Spanish Crown, and among his rights and duties were the right of granting pardons; the right to suspend resolutions passed by the Spanish government if he found them inapplicable to Puerto Rico; and emergency powers under which he could suspend constitutional guarantees and declare a state of martial law. To assist the governor general there was a cabinet composed of a president, a secretary of Government and Justice, and secretaries of the Treasury, Education, Public Works, and Agriculture. Under the law, all cabinet members were required to be Puerto Rican.

Legislative powers were exercised by a two-house parliament called the Insular Assembly. Though the two houses were supposed to be equal in power, each was differently constituted. The lower house, called the Chamber of Representatives, was composed of members elected popularly for five-year terms on the basis of one representative for every twenty-five thousand inhabitants. To be eligible for office as a representative a man had to be of legal age and either have been born in Puerto Rico or have lived in the island continuously for four years prior to his election.

The upper house was called the Administrative Council and was composed of fifteen members. Eight of the members were elected; of the eight, half were replaced every five years. The other seven members were appointed to life terms by the governor general. Administrative council members had to be at least thirty-five years old and had to qualify under the same residence rules as representatives.

Legislature members were elected by popular

vote. All Puerto Rican males over twenty-five years of age were eligible to vote without regard to race, education, or property. Women were not allowed to vote.

Among the matters subject to legislation by the Insular Assembly were the island's administrative organization, public health and sanitation, banking and public credit, public education, and the monetary system. It had the power to regulate tariffs, provide for the island's budget and revenues, and to negotiate commercial treaties with foreign governments—though commercial treaties were subject to review by the Spanish government. The Insular Assembly received the governor general's oath of office and also had the power to impeach cabinet members.

From the standpoint of Puerto Rican self-government, the most obvious shortcoming of this system was that the governor general was still imposed on Puerto Rico by a foreign political body. And by the governor general's right to appoint seven of the fifteen members of the administrative council the separation between the executive and legislative branches of government was weakened.

Under the new autonomous government the already existing judicial system remained essentially unchanged. At the lowest level was a system of municipal courts, then a system of district courts and finally, over all, were three *Audiencias* or superior courts. Appeals could be carried from the *Audiencias* to the Supreme Court of Spain.

In the light of Puerto Rico's subsequent history, several things about the Autonomous Charter seem especially important. The charter bound Spain as well as Puerto Rico to the terms of their relationship, which was declared unalterable except by petition of the Insular Assembly. In other words, Spain legally gave up much of the power it had always claimed to hold over Puerto Rico—power under which it could regulate and control the island and its people in any way it saw fit. Then, the governor general had to take his oath of office before the Puerto Rican Insular Assembly, swearing his responsibility to the people of Puerto Rico as well as to the king and government of Spain. All government officers other than the governor general were to be Puerto Ricans. And Puerto Rico had the right to trade freely with the world at large and had very broad powers to regulate the terms of that trade. Lastly, to counterbalance the fact that in some ways Puerto Rico would continue to be dependent on Spain, the Puerto Rican people could elect delegates to both houses of the Spanish Cortes, where they had full voting rights.

Neither Governor General Macias nor the Puerto Rican political leaders delayed in moving to establish the new Puerto Rican government authorized by the Autonomous Charter. But even as the campaigns for electoral office got under way, events beyond Puerto Rico's shores and outside of Puerto Rican control were taking place that would end by frustrating Puerto Rican hopes of enjoying the newly recognized right to self-government. In the United States, the press was rousing public sentiment in favor of war with Spain over the issue of Spanish action in Cuba, where Cuban independence fighters sought to end their colonial relation to Spain. Strongly worded diplomatic exchanges passed between Spain and the United States and, as tensions between those two nations mounted, Puerto Rican steps toward establishing its government turned out to be a futile counterpoint to the maneuvers of much greater forces.

In March 1898 the people of Puerto Rico elected their first representatives to the newly constituted Insular Assembly. The next month the United States declared war on Spain. Governor General Macias suspended the guarantees of the Autonomous Charter and declared a state of emergency in fear of an attack by the United States. His fear was proved well founded, for in mid-May a United States naval fleet appeared off San Juan and shelled the city for several hours. Little damage was done and no attempt at a landing was made. But wartime tension heightened on the island, and trade—on which the people of Puerto Rico depended for a large part of their food supply—was in a chaotic state. Still, even in the midst of these conditions, the commitment of Governor General Macias and of the Puerto Ricans to the principles of the Autonomous Charter was clear. Instead of consolidating his emergency powers, Governor

General Macias relaxed them, and in July 1898 permitted the newly elected Insular Assembly to meet and to take up its duties as the representative legislature of the Puerto Rican people. Just one week later, Puerto Rico was invaded by military troops of the United States, and Puerto Rico's autonomous government was dead almost at its birth.

Much has been written about the circumstances that led to the Spanish-American War and of the motives of those who provoked it. But whatever the interpretation given to those factors, one thing seems quite clear: the Spanish-American War climaxed a century of United States expansion into territories that had once been claimed by Spain. The territory that comprised the Louisiana Purchase; Florida; Texas; all the lands of the Southwest and California ceded to the United States as the price of peace in its war with Mexico—all had been Spanish possessions. The United States interest in Spain's Caribbean possessions, especially Cuba, goes back at least to the time when Thomas Jefferson was Secretary of State. With the acquisition of Spanish Florida and Cuba, Jefferson felt, the United States would have reached its natural limits to the south and east.

During the nineteenth century, United States policy was to see that Cuba and Puerto Rico, at least, remained under Spanish control until such time as the United States could take possession. Fears were expressed that should Cuba or Puerto

Rico become independent they might be annexed by England, the principal rival of the United States for control of American shipping and commerce in the nineteenth century. Or, if they did not fall to England, their own independence would be a stumbling block for United States plans to annex them.

In the 1820s, when Mexico and Venezuela— both newly independent of Spain—planned a joint expedition to drive Spain's soldiers from Cuba and Puerto Rico, the United States opposed the plan vigorously enough to cause it to be abandoned. In the years that followed the United States tried more than once to get Spain to sell its Caribbean possessions. Spain steadfastly refused. Then, in the 1850s, the Ostend Manifesto asserted that the United States had the right to take Cuba by force if Spain would not sell. The theory behind the Ostend Manifesto was that the United States needed Cuba in order to protect its national interests, and since it needed it, it had the right to take it. There was no doubt that what the United States could justify for itself on the grounds of national interest with respect to Cuba could be applied to Puerto Rico as well.

At the end of the nineteenth century, the United States appears to have decided that the time for waiting was past. From about 1896 on it began to claim the right to interest itself in the Cuban war for independence, and United States newspapers stirred up their readers' sentiment for a war with

Spain. No evidence of Spain's willingness to make concessions in the Caribbean was enough to prevent a war with the United States that Spain did not want, stood to gain little and to lose much by, and had little hope of winning. In 1898 the U.S.S. *Maine* blew up in Havana harbor, and on the crest of popular emotion which blamed Spain for that tragedy the United States declared war on Spain. When that short war was over, the United States had gained possession of Cuba, of Puerto Rico, and of the Philippine Islands.

The war in Puerto Rico was brief. The naval bombardment of San Juan in May of 1898 has already been mentioned. Then, on July 25, 1898, 3,400 United States troops commanded by General Nelson A. Miles landed at Guanica, not far from where Columbus had first stepped ashore, and in a brief battle they defeated the Spanish troops that were defending Yauco, a short distance inland. Two days later the defenseless city of Ponce surrendered to another body of troops commanded by General George Wilson, who then began the march across the central highway toward San Juan. In the mountains, not far beyond Coamo, General Wilson's advance was stopped for three days by Spanish soldiers. But before that contest was finally decided one way or another the order came to cease fire. Spain had surrendered, and Puerto Rico was in the hands of an armed invader for the first time since Ponce de León defeated the Taínos nearly four hundred years before. All in all, sixteen thousand United States soldiers had invaded Puerto Rico against a Spanish force of about eight thousand soldiers. There were no major battles and few casualties.

But it would be wrong to leave the impression that Spain surrendered to the United States without a real struggle. In the battles for Cuba and the Philippine Islands Spain's Atlantic and Pacific fleets were destroyed by the more modern and powerful United States fleets, and in both those islands the fighting on land was fierce and bloody. Too, in both the Philippine Islands and in Cuba, there were large independence armies fighting against Spain, as well as United States soldiers. It was Puerto Rico's fortune not to be the battlefield on which the war between the Spanish and the Anglo-American nations was decided. The war was nearly over by the time United States troops landed in Puerto Rico.

The people of Puerto Rico did not rise up in arms to stop the United States troops from landing on the island. Spanish and *criollo* loyalists belonged principally to the "upper classes" which rely on armies to do their fighting; when Spain surrendered, so did they. The Autonomists seemed to fear little from the United States. They had just wrung a recognition of their island's rights from the Spanish monarchy, after all, and they expected even more freedom from association with the United States, whose government and spokesmen proclaimed it the most liberal in the world. For the separatists, the United States victory over Spain seemed tantamount to their own victory. Many Puerto Rican separatists were in Cuba, fighting against Spain in the Cuban revolutionary army. With United States newspapers stirring up their readers with sympathetic accounts of the heroic revolutionary struggle in Cuba and with horror stories of the atrocities committed by Spanish troops, it was perfectly natural to suppose that the United States was committed to Cuban and Puerto Rican independence. Certainly that was the impression and belief of the Cuban and Puerto Rican revolutionary party in New York which furnished the United States government with maps and descriptions of Puerto Rico's defenses in order to facilitate the invasion. And in Puerto Rico, far from opposing the United States troops, separatists in San Germán seized the town and threw out the old municipal government.

The attitudes with which most Puerto Ricans seem to have anticipated the United States invasion appeared to be justified at first. On July 28, three days after the landing at Guanica, General Miles issued a proclamation:

> Headquarters of the Army
> Ponce, P. R., July 28, 1898
>
> To the Inhabitants of Puerto Rico:
>   In the prosecution of the war against the Kingdom of Spain by the people of the United States in the cause of liberty, justice, and humanity, its military forces have come to occupy the island of Puerto Rico. They come

bearing the banner of freedom, inspired by a noble purpose to seek the enemies of our country and yours, and to destroy or capture all who are in armed resistance. They bring you the fostering arm of a nation of free people, whose greatest power is in justice and humanity to all those living within its fold. Hence, the first effect of this occupation will be the immediate release from your former political relations, and it is hoped a cheerful acceptance of the Government of the United States. The chief object of the American military forces will be to overthrow the armed authority of Spain and to give to the people of your beautiful island the largest measure of liberty consistent with this military occupation. We have not come to make war upon the people of a country that for centuries has been oppressed, but on the contrary, to bring you protection, not only to yourselves but to your property, to promote your prosperity, and to bestow upon you the immunities and blessing of the liberal institutions of our Government. It is not our purpose to interfere with any existing laws and customs that are wholesome or beneficial to your people so long as they conform to the rules of military administration, of order and justice. This is not a war of devastation, but one to give all within the control of its military and naval forces the advantages and blessings of enlightened civilization.

NELSON A. MILES
Major-General, Commanding U.S. Army[1]

The next day General Miles expressed himself again, but this time in a circular letter issued over the signature of J. C. Gilmore, Brigadier General, which communicated to subordinate commanding officers instructions that "will govern you or your successor in the discharge of your duties relating to the military government of the territory now occupied or hereafter to be occupied by the United States forces under your command."

The tone of these instructions was somewhat different from that of the proclamation to the Puerto Rican people. In both, the general referred to ending the Puerto Rican's former political relations (without even noticing, apparently, that this included their relations with their own island government which they had so recently elected), but whereas in the proclamation the ending of "former political relations" was associated with "the fostering arm of a nation of free people," the letter to the generals read:

> The effect of the military occupation of the enemy's territory is the severance of the former political relations of its inhabitants, and it becomes their duty to yield obedience to the authority of the United States, the power of the military occupant being absolute and supreme and immediately operating upon the political conditions of the inhabitants.[2]

But the commanding general was not interested in abusing that absolute authority, for he went on to direct that "municipal laws, in so far as they affect the private rights of persons and property and provide for the punishment of crime, should be continued in force as far as they are compatible with the new order of things. . . ." Except that "under no circumstances shall the criminal courts exercise jurisdiction over any crime or offense committed by any person belonging to the Army or person serving with it . . . nor over any crime or offense committed on either of the same by any inhabitant. . . ."[2]

Almost immediately after the cease-fire order of August 14, General Miles left the island, turning over command of the United States forces in Puerto Rico to General John R. Brooke. Spain began the evacuation of its forces and effected the formal transfer of power to the United States. On October 16, 1898, the Spanish governor general of Puerto Rico left the island. Two days later the flag of Spain was lowered from the place it had occupied for so long above El Morro fortress. Puerto Rico was established as a military geographical department under the United States War Department, and General Brooke became Puerto Rico's first United States military governor.

General Brooke was more modest than his successors were to be in restructuring Puerto Rican institutions. He limited himself to such measures as abolishing the Puerto Rican Court of Appeals and substituting the Supreme Court of the United States; abolishing the Insular Assembly, while leaving in office the executive cabinet; and abolishing the use of stamped paper for legal communications. But even under General Brooke, Puerto Rico's separatists began to show concern as the United States Army settled down to take over the island's administration. In the United States, the Cuban and Puerto Rican revolutionary party was being almost completely ignored, now that the fighting was over. In Cuba, United States officials were insisting that the Cuban revolutionary army, which had fought Spain unaided for three years before the United States entered the war, should be disbanded and disarmed. And when the military government of General Brooke was announced in Puerto Rico, an active campaign was begun to prevent the United States from making a colonial possession of it. Just five days after General Brooke was named military governor, the opposition League of Patriots was formed under the leadership of Eugenio María de Hostos, a Puerto Rican patriot and international revolutionary.

De Hostos was born in Mayagüez, Puerto Rico, in 1839. Educated on the island and in Spain, he struggled for the autonomy of Cuba and Puerto Rico, and for an end to slavery, in the early 1860s. Later he became convinced that self-determination for Puerto Rico and Cuba was not possible unless the islands were independent, and he left the island to join with more revolutionary elements. In New York he edited the official newspaper of the Cuban revolutionaries, *La Revolución*. When Cuba's ten-year war for independence ended in apparent failure, de Hostos moved to Chile, where he became active in the cause of women's rights. In 1874 he moved to the Dominican Republic, where he published *Las tres Antillas*, a publication dedicated to the ideal of an Antillean Confederation that would unite Cuba, Santo Domingo, and

Puerto Rico. But when his own land, Puerto Rico, came under the military control of the United States de Hostos returned.

The first objective of the League of Patriots was to have the military government replaced by civil government. Then, as alternative solutions to the question of Puerto Rico's relationship to the United States, de Hostos argued that only two were possible. Either the United States could admit Puerto Rico into its Union as a free state equal to the others, or Puerto Rico must be independent. As an immediate measure, he sought a plebiscite that would allow the people of Puerto Rico to choose between annexation and independence. But annexation, on any other basis than full statehood, could be only a temporary measure leading to independence. De Hostos and the League of Patriots were not popular with the military government, nor with many of the upper-class elite interested in maintaining cordial relations with the occupying forces. De Hostos was not able to organize the massive movement with which he hoped to challenge the military government by legal means. José Luis Vivas writes in *Historia de Puerto Rico* that when de Hostos died in 1903 "the man whom three nations claimed as son left his own nation prostrate: neither province, nor state, nor territory."[3]

The terms of peace between the United States and Spain were agreed to in the Treaty of Paris which was signed on December 10, 1898, and then

returned to the Spanish and United States governments for ratification. Under the treaty terms,
Spain gave up the Philippines, Guam, Cuba, and
Puerto Rico to the United States. In return for the
cession of the Philippine archipelago Spain received a $20 million indemnity from the United
States. The treaty was formulated without consult-
ing any member of Puerto Rico's autonomous
government, nor were any special provisions or
responsibilities set forth relative to Puerto Rico.
The part of the treaty that bore directly on the
Puerto Rican people's future as a United States
possession was in Article IX which, after detailing
at some length the rights of Peninsula-born Spaniards living in the territory acquired by the United
States, ended by stating briefly: "The civil rights
and political status of the native inhabitants of the
territories hereby ceded to the United States shall
be determined by the Congress."[4]

The signing of the Treaty of Paris coincided
almost exactly with the appointment of a new military governor for Puerto Rico. On December 9
General Brooke was recalled and his place was
taken by General Guy V. Henry. While the United
States government moved toward ratification of
the Treaty of Paris and formal peace with Spain,
General Henry began to take concrete steps toward the restructuring of Puerto Rico, a process
that produced a conflict of cultures that is still
unresolved.

There were several elements involved in the

confrontation of Puerto Ricans with the military forces of the United States that made the relationship problematic. It is doubtful if any people likes to be ruled by force, and many Puerto Ricans who expressed themselves on the subject felt as if they had been forced backward to the time when Spain's military governor generals with unlimited power did with Puerto Rico pretty much as they wished, with the difference that at least the Spanish generals spoke a language Puerto Ricans could understand. Even those upper-class leaders and politicians who greatly admired the United States and willingly accepted a permanent union with it were eager to be rid of military government. They wanted civil government, and without question they expected that in conformity with the often avowed liberal principles of the United States that civil government would be their own. Others wanted independence, plain and simple, feeling that anything less meant a lessening of their people's dignity.

Attitudes toward the United States were complicated by economic necessity as well. There were many things, including important foods, which Puerto Rico had to obtain from outside the island. Before the Spanish-American War, Puerto Rico depended on two principal suppliers: Spain and the United States. Now Spain was beyond reach and only the United States was left. Puerto Rico depended, futher, on outside markets in which it could sell its products to earn money for the purchases it must make. Before the Spanish-American War, Puerto Rico had the same principal markets for its island products: Spain and the United States. Now only the United States was left. Even those who looked to a close union with the United States objected to doing so on the basis of economic dependency. On the other hand, those who sought independence could not easily ignore the potential economic consequences of making an enemy of the United States.

Other important elements stemmed from the cultural attitudes of the United States. The simplest name for one of them was racism. As has been described in earlier chapters, the United States first inherited from England and then developed on its own a contempt of and an animosity toward everything Spanish. Since the earliest days of the Anglo settlements in North America, Indians were treated as barely human—and many a good white Christian champion of "civilization" denied that Indians were human at all, while recognition of Black Africans' humanity was not only denied in practice in the English colonies, and then in the United States, but it was actually denied in law. In Puerto Rico the Anglo-Americans found a people whose major roots were in the African, Indian, and Spanish races and cultures. When faced with something problematic in the island, United States authorities usually assumed quite simply that whatever solution they proposed was better than any a Puerto Rican might offer. In fact, the idea that Puerto Rico should be "Americanized" for its own good seems to have been accepted among Anglo-Americans almost without question, and Puerto Rican resentment of either the premise or the process was seen as ingratitude or ignorance.

The aggressive attitude of Anglo-American free enterprise also had important consequences for the Puerto Rican – United States relations. In *Puerto Rico: Freedom and Power in the Caribbean*, Gordon K. Lewis has described the almost immediate pressures exerted on the United States government, both at home and on the island, by Anglo-American economic interests. Lewis also points out that:

> One of the first books written on the island for the American reading public, William Dinwiddie's *Porto Rico: Conditions and Possibilities*, was a frank attempt to appraise business opportunities for imaginative entrepeneurs. Another volume, Albert Gardner Robinson's *The Porto Rico of Today*, published in 1899, sought, as its main purpose, to "throw light upon the commercial possibilities in our new possession that lie within the reach of American business men."[5]

The two attitudes, of officialdom and of private enterprise, complemented each other to enforce a policy of Americanization. For United States authorities, private enterprise represented an important tool for accomplishing Americanization. For private enterprise, Americanization of the island meant a better and safer field for their endeavors.

General Henry made changes in the judicial and educational systems of Puerto Rico that were meant to make them copies of the systems developed in the United States. He also dismantled what little remained of the Puerto Rican autonomous government by abolishing the cabinet and replacing it with an executive branch of his own design (modeled after Anglo-American tradition) in which the island's administration was divided into four governmental departments, each of which was headed by an appointee of his own. To safeguard public morals, General Henry prohibited cockfighting and abolished the lottery. To ease the burden of Puerto Rico's economic crisis, he abolished the consumer taxes on a number of important imported items, including rice, beans, and dried codfish, and he temporarily suspended the foreclosure of defaulted mortgages. To aid his troops in keeping order throughout Puerto Rico he established an insular police force controlled by the United States Army. In letters that General Henry wrote to Washington to explain his problems and his efforts in Puerto Rico, he complained that the Puerto Rican had "acquired very liberally the Spanish habit of lying and cannot be trusted." Nevertheless, in pursuit of his goal of Americanizing them, he said that he was teaching them to govern themselves, "giving them kindergarten instruction in controlling themselves without allowing them too much liberty . . . ."[5]

The Treaty of Paris was ratified on April 11,

1899, but the military government in Puerto Rico was to continue for more than another year. On May 9 General Henry was succeeded as military governor by General George W. Davis, who continued the work of preparing Puerto Rico for enlightened civilization, United States style. In August of 1899 he published a circular to explain his policies to the Puerto Rican people. He explained:

> While an arbitrary government over any territory included within the United States is not contemplated by the American Constitution and laws, under those laws it is impossible to supply any other form of governmental control than the military over territory conquered by the arms of the Union until Congress shall, by suitable enactment, determine and fix a form of civil government for such conquered territory.[6]

Until Congress should take such action, however, General Davis intended to continue the remodeling of Puerto Rico in a way that would prepare it for the kind of status he anticipated the Congress would establish, i.e., ". . . the Territorial form heretofore applied in the United States to those portions of the national domain in a transition stage or one preparatory to full statehood and membership in the Union." After detailing a number of changes that he intended to make in the island government, General Davis recognized that:

> A very considerable portion of the population calls for the institution of changes that may confer self-gov-

ernment and full autonomy. It is believed that the course being pursued will lead directly to that end by the most expeditious means possible.[6]

However, General Davis shared his countrymen's common belief in Puerto Rican inferiority. When a Puerto Rican leader suggested the formation of a Puerto Rican army battalion, General Davis agreed, but said that all officers must be Anglo-American. And in a report that General Davis made to the U.S. Congress which was holding hearings and trying to decide what course of action it should take regarding Puerto Rico, he advised strongly against allowing Puerto Ricans any real measure of self-government. The Puerto Rican people, he said, were not ready for the responsibilities of electing their own legislature, nor did they have any conception of political rights and responsibilities.

Another report on Puerto Rico was made in 1899 by Henry Carroll, who was specially appointed to investigate the Puerto Rican people and to advise Congress. In his report, Carroll observed that the major difference between Puerto Rico and Oklahoma was geographic, and that as Oklahoma had served to absorb the population overflow of surrounding states so Puerto Rico would provide a field for United States capital and enterprises. Prosperity in Puerto Rico, he said, "cannot be accomplished without the influx of new capital."[7]

His analysis of the Puerto Rican culture, however, was sympathetic. In the process of its Americanization, he recommended that special care be taken to respect valuable elements of the Spanish tradition. And he advised that Congress should grant full territorial status to Puerto Rico, with autonomous government, that would lead naturally either to full statehood or to independence.

While Congress considered the conflicting advice of Anglo-American investigators and the requests of Puerto Rican political leaders, the island was struck by a terrible hurricane, San Ciriaco. Twenty-five percent of the island population was left homeless; three thousand persons were killed; extensive damage was done to the coffee and sugar crops which were the basis of the island's economy. Emergency relief from the United States came promptly in the form of clothing and food for the homeless. But General Davis's request to Congress to authorize a $10 million bond issue, and a tax structure that would repay it, in order to undertake a serious reconstruction of the economy, was practically ignored. Only months later, Congress authorized a $200,000 relief grant for hurricane victims (instead of the reconstruction bond issue). Broken down, Congress's relief amounted to something like eighty cents a person for victims of San Ciriaco's destructive force.

Finally, Congress passed a law to end military government in Puerto Rico, but following the advice of such men as General Davis it stopped far short of recognizing Puerto Ricans' right to self-government. The Treaty of Paris, Congress maintained, had given it the right to deal with Puerto Rico in any way it chose. The law it passed, known as the Foraker Act, left Puerto Rico in a clearly colonial relationship to the United States though under a civil, rather than a military government. Puerto Rican leaders were surprised and bitterly disappointed; they immediately pointed out that the Foraker Act gave them much less freedom than the Autonomous Charter of 1897.

The Foraker Act gave Spaniards or nationals of other countries residing in Puerto Rico the right to choose United States citizenship. This right was not extended to the people of Puerto Rico. They were defined as just that—the People of Puerto Rico—but since Puerto Rico had no legal existence other than as a possession of the United States, its people had no genuine legal existence or representation among the nations of the world. Even their name was taken, for the United States officially changed it to Porto Rico, which has no meaning either in English or in Spanish.

The Foraker Act provided for a civil government headed by a governor and an executive cabinet, *all* of whom were appointed by the president of the United States. It is ironic that Congress protected its own rights by insisting that it must consent to presidential appointments, while the people of Puerto Rico were deprived of any voice in the matter.

A local legislature was provided for by the Foraker Act. It was composed of two houses: an upper house, called the Executive Council, and a lower house called the Chamber of Delegates. All eleven members of the Executive Council were appointed by the president of the United States. In fact, six of its members were also the governor's cabinet members. The other five members were required to be Puerto Ricans, but they, too, were presidential appointees.

The Chamber of Delegates was elected every two years by the adult males of Puerto Rico. There were thirty-five members of the Chamber; to be eligible for the office, candidates had to be at least twenty-five years of age, be able to read and write English or Spanish, and be real estate owners.

Just in case a presidentially appointed executive branch and a packed upper house in the legislature were not enough to prevent Puerto Ricans, through their lower house representation, from passing some measure of which the United States government would not approve, the Foraker Act provided ways by which such legislation could be vetoed. First, the governor could veto any Puerto Rican bill of which he did not approve. His veto could, at least theoretically, be overridden by a two-thirds majority vote in *both* upper and lower houses. If that should happen, the bill would then go to the U.S. Congress for ratification. And Congress also retained for itself the right to annul any Puerto Rican legislation of which it did not approve.

The Foraker Act also changed Puerto Rico's judicial system. A five-member Supreme Court was established over seven District Courts. The Supreme Court justices were appointed by the president of the United States, while the District Court judges were appointed by the governor. Puerto Rican Supreme Court decisions could be appealed to the Circuit Court of Boston and, ultimately, to the Supreme Court of the United States.

Puerto Rico was permitted to elect a representative known as the Resident Commissioner to the U.S. Congress where he could represent a Puerto Rican point of view but without the right to vote. To compensate for Puerto Rico's lack of participation in the federal government the island was exempted from federal taxation.

The Foraker Act had tremendous consequences for the economy of Puerto Rico. Unlike the Autonomous Charter of 1897, which provided the Puerto Rican government with broad powers to regulate its foreign trade, the Foraker Act in effect limited the island to trade with the United States. For a specified time, all goods moving from Puerto Rico to the United States or vice versa were to be taxed at 15 percent of what such goods would be taxed if they were coming into the United States from a foreign country. An exception was made of coffee, which was taxed at a higher rate. Revenues from this tax on trade went into a special fund at the disposal of the president of the United States "for the Government and benefit of Puerto Rico."

After the Puerto Rican government had organized a local tax system to provide its own revenues on the island, all taxes on trade between Puerto Rico and the United States would be dropped—again, with the exception of the tax on coffee. From then on, Puerto Rico was considered a part of the United States for trading purposes; all trade between the island and other countries would be taxed according to the protective tariffs set up by the United States to protect its own producers from foreign competition. This meant that Puerto Rico was forced to buy practically all of its external goods in the United States. Sugar, a Puerto Rican product of great interest to United States businessmen, was protected by the United States tariff wall; coffee was not.

At the time of the United States occupation of Puerto Rico, coffee was its principal crop. An important feature of the coffee cultivation was that it was done largely by growers on relatively small plantations rather than by the kind of huge *latifundia* common to sugar production. In the years prior to the United States occupation, Puerto Rican coffee had enjoyed a good position in the Spanish market and was protected by a Spanish tariff. That was a benefit that Puerto Rico lost, of course, when Spain gave up the island. Under the Foraker Act, Puerto Rico's coffee growers had to face a punitive tax on the United States market in addition to their loss of Spanish protection. Coupled to the physical damage done to coffee plantations by hurricane San Ciriaco, the trade restrictions imposed under the Foraker Act effectively destroyed the coffee industry in Puerto Rico and many small coffee growers lost their lands. Often, they became *agregados*, the semipeons who labored on and were attached to the huge sugar plantations.

The influx of Anglo-American capital foreseen and hoped for by United States officialdom took place. Its main objective was the acquisition of sugar lands, and (in spite of a law limiting land-holdings to five hundred acres, which Anglo-American investors did not scruple to violate) companies in the United States soon owned tremendous amounts of land, with the production of sugar consolidated in fewer and fewer hands. A consequence of this land concentration for the production of sugar was that much land which had been used to produce food crops for the people of Puerto Rico was converted to sugar-cane production. This increased Puerto Rico's dependency on food imports, principally from the United States.

The people of Puerto Rico made it clear that they did not care for the Foraker Act, and government records as well as newspapers are full of expressions to that effect. Not only was Puerto Rican self-government almost a fiction, but the governors and other officials appointed from the United States to rule the island were often appointed to their posts in repayment for political favors to the party in power in the United States. With the Puerto Rican legislature almost powerless, many Puerto Ricans deeply concerned with their island's problems saw governmental participation as futile; the legislature and government inevitably attracted self-seekers interested in personal privilege, while honest legislators were frustrated at finding themselves part of a figurehead government.

In 1909-10, however, the Chamber of Delegates rebelled. The one presumably real responsibility that the lower house had was to appropriate funds for the island government and administration. In the year mentioned, the Chamber of Delegates tried to use this power as a lever to force some changes from the U.S. Congress. The Puerto Ricans refused to approve a budget for the coming year until their grievances were heard and considered. The U.S. Congress, however, simply passed a law carrying the previous year's budget into effect for the new year, thus proving that it could and would legislate for Puerto Rico itself whenever it felt it was necessary.

Sentiment for independence grew in Puerto Rico, though there were still those who wanted to see Puerto Rico become a state within the Union. In fact, those two positions were not so opposed as they might seem. Puerto Ricans expressed more than anything else a desire to be masters in their own island, and at the time the self-government of a state within the Union was much more real than what they had. That fact, coupled with the one that both unionists and separatists were for the most part agreed that some transitional stage would have to be accepted, often made political positions difficult to distinguish. During this time Luis Muñoz Rivera, the compromiser who on his own had reached the understanding with Sagasta in Spain that had led to the Autonomous Charter, went his own way again to try to resolve the problem of Puerto Rico's relationship with the United States. As head of the *Partido Unión*, whose eventual goal was independence but which sought autonomy as immediate goal, Muñoz Rivera obtained the post of Resident Commissioner in Washington in order to learn United States politics at first hand and from a "practical" viewpoint. Perhaps it was because of that practical experience that he began to raise his voice less loudly for independence and that he even convinced his party to shrink its independence plank in order to win more immediate self-government for his people.

The Foraker Act had been defined in its title as a temporary measure, and by 1917 the continued pressure of Puerto Rican political leaders and of a few supporters in the U.S. Congress resulted in its substitution by a new Organic Act known as the Jones Act.

One important provision of the Jones Act gave Puerto Ricans United States citizenship. At the same time, by including in the Jones bill a special Bill of Rights, the U.S. Congress pointed up its contention that even the granting of citizenship to Puerto Ricans did not confer on them all the rights of the Constitution of the United States. Repeatedly, in years to come, the United States Supreme Court would uphold the position of Congress on that point.

A measure of the change in the Puerto Rican attitude toward the United States was that by 1917 the prospect of United States citizenship no longer had the support among Puerto Ricans that it had at the beginning of the occupation. Proponents of independence argued that citizenship was meant to tie them irrevocably to the United States. Others maintained that it was simply a maneuver to legalize the drafting of Puerto Rican men into the United States Army. Statehood advocates agreed that citizenship bound Puerto Rico closer to the United States. Their disagreement with the Jones Act was that in it the United States had not committed itself to eventual statehood for Puerto Rico. To urge their position, however, they argued that by granting citizenship the United States had, in fact, committed itself to granting statehood.

In "A Historical Survey of the Puerto Rico Status Question, 1898-1965," prepared for the United States – Puerto Rico Commission on the Status of Puerto Rico, 1966, Professor Robert J. Hunter describes in some detail the struggle and frustration of Puerto Ricans trying to get the United States to honor its own democratic principles in relation to their island. On the citizenship issue, Hunter writes:

In the hearings on the Jones bill, delegations from the majority Unionist Party of Puerto Rico [*Partido Unión de Puerto Rico*] had expressed a preference for the designation "citizen of Puerto Rico." They claimed that a substantial number of their fellow citizens would reject American citizenship if it were offered. During the floor debate, Resident Commissioner Muñoz Rivera expressed the same point of view, and suggested that a plebiscite be held to determine whether or not Puerto Ricans still desired American citizenship. . . . An explanation of this seeming reversal of Puerto Rican opinion requires some consideration of the internal pressures of the insular political parties. . . . The Union Party's original platform had considered statehood, independence or full local autonomy under the American flag as acceptable status choices. As the years passed and reforms seemed impossible to obtain, the once-small independence wing of the Unionist Party, led by fiery orator José de Diego, gained strength. The stinging rebukes flung at the island during the 1909 legislative crisis [which the Puerto Rican legislature precipitated by refusing to pass an island budget in order to force Congress to pay some attention to Puerto Rico's demands] and the continued indifference of the Administration to Puerto Rican demands piqued the latent nationalism of even the most moderate islanders. Many came to feel that both the cultural and political integrity of the island required that American influence be kept at arm's length. One manifestation of this point of view was to resist American citizenship. . . . Perhaps even more basic to the confusing testimonies on the citizenship feature of the Jones bill was the fact that over the years, Congress had been partially misinformed regarding Puerto Rican feelings on this issue. The Republican Party of Puerto Rico and the labor

movement (which organized the Socialist Party in 1915)
were ardent supporters of American citizenship. Both
of these groups had strong friends in Washington who
supplemented the pro-citizenship memorials sent by
the islanders. But the Republicans and the Labor-
Socialist groups clearly constituted a minority in insular
politics. They did not win an island-wide election from
1904 through 1920, and their few representatives in
the House of Delegates were unable to check the activities of the overwhelming Union majorities. Thus, while
the pro-citizenship parties received much attention in
Washington, they spoke for only a minority of the people in the island.[8]

Another factor in the "seeming reversal of Puerto Rican opinion" about United States citizenship
since 1898, not mentioned by Professor Hunter,
but reiterated by such spokesmen for Puerto Rican
independence as José de Diego[9], was the Puerto
Ricans' awareness of repeated military interven-
tions by the United States in the independent
Republic of Cuba, and of armed invasions and
occupations by United States military forces of the
independent Republics of Mexico, Nicaragua, Haiti, and the Dominican Republic.

In any event, Congress decided that Puerto Ricans should have United States citizenship. It
claimed the right to legislate for Puerto Rico as it
saw fit, and so it simply passed a law declaring that
all Puerto Ricans were United States citizens. Apparently not wanting to appear as autocratic as it
claimed the right to be, it conferred citizenship in
such a way as to make it appear that the choice was

Puerto Rican. That is, it gave the individual citizens of Puerto Rico the right to reject citizenship if they should choose to do so. Such persons had to make a formal declaration of rejection and to accept the loss of important political rights. Apologists for United States policy in Puerto Rico point to the small number of people who refused citizenship as proof that most people wanted it. Opponents point to the consequences of rejecting citizenship and claim that its refusal by *any* Puerto Ricans shows how unpopular the idea was.

The Jones Act did provide for a more liberal organization of the Puerto Rican government. The Executive Council, all of whose members were presidential appointees, was replaced by a Senate of nineteen members elected by the people. Puerto Rican legislation was still subject to veto by the governor; if that veto were overridden the president of the United States could veto. Congress, of course, retained the right to annul any Puerto Rican legislation. Puerto Rico remained an unincorporated territory of the United States with no more rights than Congress might choose to allow.

If Congress had hoped that the concessions of the Jones Act would satisfy the people of Puerto Rico they were mistaken. Hunter writes of the new generation of men who had been children when the United States invaded their island:

> For such men, the Jones bill was not enough. The permanent status of Puerto Rico was still unresolved.

Its resolution seemed as far away as ever. Despite the provisions for a popularly elected legislature, there was still a veto power vested in a mainland-appointed governor, in a president in whose election they played no part, and in a U.S. Congress in which they had no vote. They were subject to be drafted to fight in a war to make the world safe for democracy, to secure the right to self-determination for others, when they felt they lacked those privileges for themselves.[10]

Such men would not sit idly by and wait for the day when Congress, moved by some impulse of its own, volunteered to give up its authority over the island. Puerto Ricans used every means at their disposal to make their needs, their desires, and their complaints known to their governor and to the United States government. The prevailing response from United States politicians (encouraged by Anglo-American business interests either profiting from the Puerto Rican situation or afraid of the competition that might follow on resolution of its status) was one of anger at what they called Puerto Rican ingratitude. Typical expressions of United States impatience with Puerto Rican demands are the following:

Representative Joseph G. Cannon, visiting Puerto Rico in 1919: "Why are you worrying about Statehood or Independence? You will get either or both just as soon as you are ready."[11]

Chairman Horace M. Towner of the House Insular Affairs Committee, in a letter addressed to the Puerto Rican legislature, in 1920:

Friends of Puerto Rico will soon find it impossible to help the island if this propaganda is continued. I assure you that there is not now, and there is not likely to be, any considerable sentiment in this country for the independence of Puerto Rico. There is a legitimate ground for a larger measure of self-government, but that has been greatly injured by the active independence propaganda.[12]

Governor of Puerto Rico E. Montgomery Reily, in his inaugural speech, in 1921: "Neither, my friends, is there any room on this island for any flag other than the Stars and Stripes. So long as Old Glory waves over the United States, it will continue to wave over Puerto Rico."[13]

And in a letter written by Reily a few days later to Antonio Barceló, president of the Puerto Rican Senate on the subject of governmental appointments:

. . . I want you to fully understand that I shall never appoint any man to any office who is an advocate of independence. When you publicly renounce independence and break loose from your pernicious and un-American associates, then I will be glad to have your recommendations.[14]

The response of Puerto Ricans to the United States attitude that sought to banish any expression of independence sentiment was the formation of the Nationalist party. Its roots were in the unsuccessful Antillean Union, founded in 1915 by José de Diego, and the equally unsuccessful Nationalist Association of Ponce and its District, founded in 1917. But in 1922, under the leadership of José Coll y Cuchi and José de Diego, a great assembly of Puerto Rican people at Río Piedras proclaimed Puerto Rico's right to be a free Republic and united to form the Nationalist party. From then on, Puerto Rican voters would no longer be limited to sorting out the ambiguous political positions of the traditional parties in regard to the status question. The Nationalist party maintained that Puerto Rico had been illegally invaded and acquired by the United States, inasmuch as it had at that time already constituted its own autonomous government. The United States should get out of Puerto Rico, the Nationalists maintained, and Puerto Rico should be free.

7

A QUESTION OF STATUS

CLOSELY LINKED TO the political issues raised by
United States control of Puerto Rico were changes
in the functioning of the Puerto Rican economy.
United States control of Puerto Rico was accompanied by a marked increase in economic activity
during approximately the first thirty years. By
1910 about $10 million of private capital from the
United States had been invested in sugar-cane
fields and mills alone. Sugar exports, which had
averaged 57,000 tons per year during the last
years of Spanish rule, rose to 489,000 tons in
1917. Luis Muñoz Marín, son of Luis Muñoz Rivera and destined to become one of the most influential Puerto Rican leaders of his time, wrote about
"Porto Rico: The American Colony" in 1924. Dis-
cussing the growth of the sugar industry, Muñoz
Marín described the growing centralization of
sugar production (several hundred sugar mills at

the turn of the century; seventy-five mills in 1920) and acknowledged the tremendous increase in sugar production which had accompanied that centralization:

> That is the open glory of the colonialists. Profit has been known to surpass 100 percent per annum, and a very large share of it leaves the island never to return. That is the secret glory of the colonialists. And even this ghastly spectacle of wealth drained from a starving population into the richest country on earth is sanctimoniously set down in the official reports as a "favorable trade balance."[1]

Favorable to the United States, of course. For the Puerto Rican laborers who grew and cut and milled the sugar, the impressive increase recorded in statistical charts under "Gross National Product" meant very little. Muñoz Marín wrote that: "the average daily wage paid to a laborer in the cane-fields is about a dollar, with a six months working year, when prices for such necessities of life as he consumes are slightly higher than in New York." Nor was the sugar-cane worker atypical of what was happening on the island as a whole, for "the business manager of one of the principal newspapers in San Juan, a peculiarly capable and reliable man, received until recently a monthly salary of one hundred dollars for a task that rarely released him before nine o'clock at night."

By 1930 private corporations in the United States were the absentee owners of 60 percent of

Puerto Rican banking and public utilities; 80 percent of the tobacco industry; 60 percent of the sugar industry; and 100 percent of the steamship lines that carried goods between Puerto Rico and the United States. Four absentee corporations owned 46 percent of all lands worked for sugar.

Henry Wells, whose *The Modernization of Puerto Rico* is far from being a partisan attack on United States policies in Puerto Rico, writes that during the first thirty years of United States occupation the government in Washington was "largely indifferent to the poverty of the islanders." Wells cites wages that match in their inadequacy those cited by Muñoz Marín and concludes that:

> . . . it seems likely that the condition of the working classes had not substantially improved during the first thirty years of American control. It may indeed have worsened, for the rapid growth in population (up from 953,000 in 1899 to 1,544,000 in 1930, a sixty-one percent increase) does not seem to have been accompanied by a corresponding rise in real income or employment opportunities. Moreover, the inexorable enlargement of the cane fields deprived many a small farmer and *agregado* of the plots on which they had raised part of their food supply.[2]

The picture drawn so far in this chapter reflects Puerto Rican conditions during the postwar years of the 1920s when Puerto Rico could have expected to benefit most from its relations with the booming United States economy. But efforts of

Puerto Rican legislators to effect a more even distribution of the money earned by the island's sugar cane often were frustrated by the Anglo-American governor and administrators sent from Washington. For example, in 1921 the Puerto Rican legislature passed a law under which a system of government-owned railroads would be built in order to allow small sugar planters to sell their cane to whatever mill would pay the best price. Some $14 million in loans were authorized to put the law into effect, but Governor Reily simply refused to issue the loans. Reily's successor, Governor Horace M. Towner, was less obviously autocratic in his refusal. His way of handling the matter was to push for a $6 million loan to finance building projects less objectionable to the big sugar interests—and then to point out that this loan raised the public debt just past the point that would allow a $14 million loan to be made within the legal public debt limit. The U.S. Congress has authority to define the allowable federal debt for the United States, and state legislatures define their own acceptable public debt, but Puerto Rico's limit is defined for it in a legislature not its own.

Obviously, since Puerto Rico's civil governors had very broad direct powers in the island, and an influence with the United States government much greater than that of Puerto Rican political leaders, the quality of government in the island was directly related to the quality and the competence of the men appointed to govern. Although numerous

writers in the United States have referred to the
general competence and sincerity of these men,
none of the fifteen Anglo-American civilians who
have governed Puerto Rico learned to speak Spanish well, if at all. An interesting view of Anglo-
American governors, counter to the generally
favorable one, is suggested by Kal Wagenheim in
Puerto Rico: A Profile:

> In 1935, anger over the ineptness of one governor
> prompted Puerto Ricans to bomb his home and send
> letters to Washington petitioning his ouster. Another
> governor caused a drunken row at a White House con-
> cert and was shipped back to Puerto Rico to complete
> his term of office. Another, accused in the mainland
> press of improper action, forged a letter, using the
> name of a prominent Puerto Rican, and sent it to the
> press to defend himself. Another, asked by a Senate
> committee for his credentials as an administrator, re-
> plied that in his hometown he had once run a 5- and
> 10-cent store.[3]

Inept or unconcerned government on the part
of the United States and its local appointees; an
enforced economic relationship with the United
States that left the island vulnerable to exploitation
by private Anglo-American business interests; a
balance of trade that was regularly out of balance
in favor of the United States; poverty, malnutri-
tion, disease, and illiteracy commonplace among
Puerto Rico's people: these were a major part of
Puerto Rico's experience during the booming
1920s. At the end of the decade, Puerto Rico's

plight was so desperate that when, in 1928, Charles Lindbergh visited the island its leaders persuaded him to take a message back with him to the United States. The message was addressed to President Coolidge and was both brief and simple: "Grant us the freedom that you enjoy, for which you struggled, which you worship, which we deserve, and you have promised us." In addition, a cablegram to President Coolidge reinforced this message and detailed Puerto Rican grievances.

President Coolidge was so angered at the Puerto Rican message that he answered in a letter to Governor Towner which was later made public. President Coolidge denied the charges made against the United States and insisted that the island's present government was the most liberal it had ever known. He said that the United States had given Puerto Rico a ". . . greater liberty than it has ever enjoyed and powers of government for the exercise of which its people are barely prepared. . . ." Clearly, the President of the United States expected gratitude rather than demands for independence from the United States citizens of Puerto Rico.

Not only were the last years of the 1920s difficult for Puerto Rico because of the tensions of its political relations with the United States, but they brought natural and economic catastrophes to the island as well. In 1928 the hurricane San Felipe struck Puerto Rico with winds in excess of two hundred miles per hour. Half a million people were left without homes; the already seriously crippled coffee industry was virtually wiped out; $85 million worth of material damage was done; thousands were hurt; and 312 persons died.

The next year, 1929, the United States stock market crashed and the Great Depression began. The boom years of the twenties were over for the United States. For Puerto Rico, closely linked to the United States economy, and barely able to survive even during one of the most affluent periods in the United States, the depression brought hardships that are almost incalculable.

The political setbacks, natural catastrophe, and economic crisis with which the 1920s closed were reflected in the swift growth of Puerto Rico's Nationalist party during the decade that followed. In 1930 the Nationalist party leadership was assumed by Pedro Albizu Campos. He was an honors graduate of Harvard, where he took degrees in both law and chemical engineering, and he served with distinction as an officer in the United States Army during World War I. In 1922 his political views had been conservative enough for him to disagree with the founding of the Nationalist party, but his experiences in Puerto Rican politics convinced him both of the necessity of Puerto Rican independence and of the futility of expecting to receive it at the hands of the United States except through genuine struggle. A long tour of other Latin American countries also made clear to him the essentially colonialist attitude of the United States toward other American nations, and after his return to Puerto Rico he began to work effectively to organize his people's sentiment for independence.

A compelling speaker, Albizu Campos denounced the United States economic exploitation of the island and insisted that it had no legal right to be there. The present status of Puerto Rico, he maintained, was one imposed by the force of arms and if necessary the use of force was justified to remove it. This was hardly a point of view calculated to gain support from Puerto Rico's governors or from the politicians whose hopes—and personal careers—depended on the United States eventually granting genuine self-government for Puerto Rico whether on the basis of independence, statehood, or autonomy.

In 1932 the Nationalist party participated for the first time in a Puerto Rican election, but with small success at the polls. Convinced of the futility of trying to work "within the system" of colonial government, the Nationalist party began to organize on more militant lines. A Puerto Rican Republic was declared and Nationalist youth began to learn military drill—principally with wooden rifles. Albizu Campos and other speakers denounced the established parties as collaborators; they described the electoral processes in the island as fraudulent; and they urged Puerto Ricans to express their desire for independence by boycotting elections. At a demonstration before the Capitol in 1932 a crowd of Nationalists tried to enter the legislative chambers. There was a scuffle with police, a stairway broke, and one person died. A dozen more were injured.

Another election in 1932, meanwhile, proved of importance to Puerto Rico. In the United States, Franklin Delano Roosevelt was elected to the presidency on a platform that promised a New Deal and an end to the depression. Roosevelt promised a new era of friendship toward Latin American countries in his famous Good Neighbor policy. With the promise of the federal government that it would use its resources to remedy economic problems, many people in Puerto Rico recovered their hope. The new administration permitted the island to abandon officially the name Porto Rico. A commission to investigate conditions in Puerto Rico was sent, and conferences were held with Puerto Rican experts and scholars to hear their views on Puerto Rico's needs.

Roosevelt's appointments to the island's governorship, however, proved little better than any of their predecessors. In 1933 Robert Hayes Gore was appointed. A Southerner with strong racial prejudices, Gore was also determined to discourage any sentiment for independence. When making appointments of Puerto Ricans to any island post, Gore would first require the appointee to sign a letter of resignation, leaving only the date blank to be filled in by Gore if and when the official displeased him. Gore was not well liked; in less than a year the Puerto Ricans were able to force his resignation.

Gore's successor was General Blanton Winship,

a retired army officer with little interest in Puerto Rico's problems. They could all be cured, he seemed to feel, if Puerto Rico would concentrate on making the island attractive to tourists. His one other serious commitment was to the overhauling of the insular police along United States Army lines.

But efforts to deal with the island's economic problems were made. In 1933 the Puerto Rican Emergency Reconstruction Administration (known as *la Prera* in the island) was set up with federal funds. It administered a public works and relief program, and without any question brought needed relief to Puerto Ricans who were literally starving. But none of the projects that it undertook attacked the basic problems of Puerto Rico's poverty. Much money was wasted through bureaucratic ineffi-ciencies and political jealousies and its best results (beyond providing much needed hunger relief) were in repairing buildings damaged by the hurri-canes of 1928 and 1932 and in the construction of some school and hospital buildings.

Meanwhile, a genuine reconstruction plan was formulated by Carlos Chardón, chancellor of the University; Rafael Fernández Garcia, a professor; and Rafaél Menéndes Ramos, the Secretary of Agriculture. Known as the Chardón Plan, it aimed at setting up a semipublic corporation that would enforce the 500-Acre Law and redistribute land among the landless poor; that would operate a government-owned sugar company as a laboratory for management-labor relations, and a cement plant as a starting point for the island's industrialization; that would develop a program of cooperatives and of security against hurricane damage; and that would develop university-level technical laboratories to train Puerto Rican technicians. The Chardón Plan was pressed on the United States government by Senator Luis Muñoz Marín, whose long residence in Washington during the years that his father was Resident Commissioner had given him a broad personal acquaintance in United States government circles. When in June 1934 President Roosevelt approved the Chardón Plan in principle, Muñoz Marín received much publicity in Puerto Rico as the man responsible for its acceptance.

But there was a large gap between acceptance in principle and acceptance in fact. In Washington, politicians and lobbyists denounced as socialist those features of the plan that might interfere with Anglo-American business habits. An Interdepartmental Committee appointed to analyze the plan did not report its findings until the middle of 1935. When it did, it rejected the land reform proposals and the idea of Puerto Rican public ownership of industry. Still, in the last half of 1935 the Puerto Rico Reconstruction Administration began to function in the island. Forty million dollars (less than half the $100 million originally estimated) was the cost estimated by the PRRA as necessary for the reconstruction of the Puerto Rican economy that Secretary of the Interior Harold L. Ickes described in a letter to Senator Duncan Fletcher that same year.

> Puerto Rico has been the victim of the *laissez faire* economy which has developed the rapid growth of great absentee-owned sugar corporations, which have absorbed much land formerly belonging to small independent growers and who in consequence have been reduced to virtual economic serfdom. While the inclusion of Puerto Rico within our tariff walls has been highly beneficial to the stockholders of those corporations, the benefits have not been passed down to the mass of Puerto Ricans. These on the contrary have seen the lands on which they formerly raised subsistence crops given over to sugar production while they have been gradually driven to import all their food staples, paying for them the high prices brought about by the tariff. There is today more widespread misery and destitution and far more unemployment in Puerto Rico than at any previous time in its history.[4]

These words written by a cabinet officer of the United States government are in marked and sad contrast to those addressed to the Puerto Rican people nearly forty years earlier by the commanding general of the United States invasion force, which promised ". . . to bring you protection, not only to yourselves but to your property, to promote your prosperity, and to bestow upon you the immunities and blessings of the liberal institutions of our Government."

Problems with the United States for Puerto Rican planners and legislators trying to restructure their island's economy were not limited to those of getting the U.S. Congress to grant aid or to pass new laws that would permit a greater economic growth. Puerto Rico's leaders also faced difficulties in trying to enforce the laws that had already been passed by the United States for the island's benefit, when such laws interfered with private United States business interests. An example is the struggle of the PRRA to enforce the 500-Acre Law against monopolist sugar companies.

In 1936 suit was brought against Rupert Hermanos, Inc., who controlled more than twelve thousand acres of sugar land in violation of both the Foraker Act and the Jones Act. The Supreme Court of Puerto Rico found against the sugar company, but the matter did not end there. The Supreme Court of Puerto Rico was inferior to the Circuit Court of Boston according to the Jones Act, and the sugar company appealed to the Boston court. In Boston, the decision of the Puerto Rican Supreme Court was reversed. This time it was the people of Puerto Rico who appealed, and the case went to the Supreme Court of the United States. Not until 1940, four years after the suit was brought, did the United States Supreme Court decide that Puerto Rico had the right to enforce a law imposed on it, in the first place, by the U.S. Congress. In the long run Puerto Rico won its case against Rupert Hermanos, but for the four years that decision was pending almost nothing could be done about other offenders. And at that time each of the four largest sugar companies in the island controlled an average of forty thousand acres.

For Puerto Rico, political and economic problems were intricately intertwined. Because of the island's relationship to the United States, economic problems with it often had to be resolved through the machinery of government and politics. On the other hand, political alterations of the Puerto Rican–United States relationship often brought economic repercussions. Within the island, too, political problems often appeared in terms of their economic consequences, and, conversely, economic upheavals produced political restlessness. The creation of the PRRA in the mid-1930s was a political attempt to deal with Puerto Rico's economic problems through government action, through the legislature, and through the courts. About the same time that the PRRA began its work, the political-economic tensions in Puerto Rico produced direct and sometimes violent demands for political change—demands that were frequently expressed in the streets. Foremost among those involved in the politics of violent confrontation were the Nationalists, though it was not always clear whether they or their opponents were responsible for the actual violence.

Late in 1935 a group of university students who opposed the Nationalist movement held a meeting, in the course of which trouble flared with a

group of pro-Nationalist youth. The police arrived, and in the fracas that followed three young
Nationalists and a spectator were killed. Albizu
Campos spoke at their funeral and stingingly denounced the Insular Police and its Anglo-American chief, E. Francis Riggs, who was the appointee
and personal friend of Governor Winship. On
February 23, 1936, two young Nationalists shot
and killed police chief Riggs. The two young men,
Hiram Rosado and Elias Beauchamp, were captured by the police and taken to police headquarters where they were beaten to death. A series of
shootings and confrontations between police and
Nationalists took place in the months that followed, as both police and Nationalists sought
vengeance. At the height of the tension, Ernest
Gruening, who was head of the PRRA, asked Senator Luis Muñoz Marín to publicly denounce the
assassination of police chief Riggs. Muñoz Marín,
who was certainly no Nationalist, replied that he
would do so if Mr. Gruening would denounce the
brutal killing of Riggs's alleged assassins. Mr.
Gruening refused.

The outrage expressed in Washington over the
death of Riggs was considerable. In an obvious
effort to teach the Puerto Ricans a lesson, Albizu
Campos, head of the Nationalist party, was arrested and tried in the Federal District Court in San
Juan. An Anglo-American prosecutor, A. Cecil
Snyder, pressed charges of sedition, illegal recruiting of soldiers, and conspiracy to incite rebellion

against Albizu Campos and eight other Nationalists. They were tried before an Anglo-American
judge, Robert A. Cooper, and finally received sen-
tences ranging from six to ten years at the federal
penitentiary at Atlanta, Georgia.

Jailing Albizu Campos did not destroy the Nationalist party in Puerto Rico, nor did it end the
flares of violence between them and the Insular
Police. The most famous — or infamous — of those
confrontations is usually referred to by Puerto
Ricans as the Ponce Massacre of 1937. Accounts of
that event are all partisan. The one that follows is
from Professor Hunter's study of the Puerto Rican
status question published by the United States –
Puerto Rico Commission on the Status of Puerto
Rico. Professor Hunter is certainly not an apolo-
gist for the Puerto Rican Nationalists.

Ever since Albizu Campos and his cohorts had been
sentenced following the Riggs assassination, Nationalists had held parades and rallies to dramatize their protests and to raise funds for legal appeals. They applied
for a permit to stage such a parade in Ponce on Palm
Sunday of 1937. The permit was first refused; then
granted; then, at the last moment revoked on orders
from the insular administration [the office of Governor
Winship]. The Nationalist demonstrators, mostly young
people, decided to proceed with the parade. As they
lined up in the square, they were faced by armed police. Suddenly, a shot rang out, and a police officer fell,
wounded. The police then began firing wildly into the
unarmed crowd. Nineteen were killed, including two
policemen, and more than 100 were injured. Reports

of the event were contradictory. Who fired the first shot is not known. Whether a result of panic or design, however, the police reaction was needlessly brutal. Most of the dead were little more than children; none were armed; many were shot in the back while seeking refuge. The overall result was a storm of wrath directed against Governor Winship and his administration. The American Civil Liberties Union investigated the affair [whereas a federal investigation followed the death of Riggs], and while they did not discount the possibility that the first shot might have come from a Nationalist hidden in the crowd, they, too, roundly castigated the police and the island administration.[5]

There were other flare-ups, including some attempts by the Nationalists to exact vengeance for their brothers who died at Ponce on that Palm Sunday. Two attempts, both failures, received much attention in the United States. In June of 1937 an attack was made on Judge Cooper, who had sentenced Albizu Campos and his fellow Nationalists. The car in which Judge Cooper was riding was riddled with bullets, but the judge somehow escaped alive. Then, on the fortieth anniversary of the United States invasion of Puerto Rico, while Governor Winship was on a reviewing stand watching a parade in celebration of that event, a group of Nationalists opened fire. Governor Winship was not injured, but a colonel of the Puerto Rican National Guard was killed as he marched in the parade.

Outrage over the violence of Nationalist resistance had combined in Washington with resentment at a number of measures taken by the PRRA to improve economic conditions for Puerto Rico. Beginning in 1937, Congress drastically reduced its appropriations for Puerto Rican reconstruction. By the end of 1938 the United States had spent $57 million during five years of New Deal dealing in Puerto Rico, including the money allocated under the old Puerto Rican Emergency Assistance scheme. The results were less than had been hoped for.

The grim picture of life for most of Puerto Rico's people had altered little by the end of the 1930s. Life expectancy was forty-six years; infant mortality from pneumonia, influenza, and intestinal diseases was still very high. Wages had actually dropped during the 1930s, until farm workers were paid as little as six cents an hour. Skilled workers might make twenty-two cents an hour—if they could find work. Diets were poor, as might be expected in a country whose per capita income was $118 per year, and which had to import much of its foodstuffs from the United States at higher than stateside prices. Only half of Puerto Rico's children attended school; only three out of ten persons were literate.

But if poverty and its attendant ills did not end with the 1930s, it seemed as if the promising political career of Muñoz Marín might be at an end. Several years of dissension between himself and Antonio Barceló, head of the Liberal party, to which Muñoz Marín belonged, ended with Muñoz

Marín's expulsion from the party. But his political failure was more apparent than real; within a short time he was to make a comeback as head of the most powerful political movement that Puerto Rico has yet known.

After his expulsion from the Liberal party, Muñoz Marín went to the rural people. It is not accurate to say that he went back, for his early life had been in Washington and then among bohemian circles in New York before his entrance into island politics. In any event, among Puerto Rico's poor he discovered that the question of Puerto Rico's political status was of less immediate concern than the question of food, land, schools, and medicine. It should be remarked, however, that Muñoz Marín's advocacy of independence was of long standing and well known, so the fact that those with whom he spoke expressed more immediate concern about more immediate issues does not necessarily mean that they did not care whether or not Puerto Rico was independent; it might just as well mean simply that they cared more about their immediate problems of poverty and disease. Muñoz Marín talked to the poor, and he listened when they talked to him. Out of those conversations came the Popular Democratic party whose symbol was the characteristic straw hat of the mountain *jíbaro* and whose motto was "Bread, Land, and Liberty."

Responding to the concerns expressed to him by the rural people, Muñoz Marín's new party addressed itself to the social and economic needs of the Puerto Rican masses rather than political status. The effectiveness of Muñoz Marín's appeal to the rural poor was demonstrated when the Popular Democratic party, which was only organized in 1938, won a majority of seats in the Senate and split the seats in the House of Representatives equally with candidates of the coalition that had controlled Puerto Rico's legislature for eight years. Muñoz Marín was returned as senator and became president of the Senate. Though this spectacular rise of the new party to power still left it with a very shaky majority in the island government, Muñoz Marín and his followers began to work for the reforms that would redeem their pledges to those who voted for them. The party platform that had won the Puerto Rican people's support called for enforcement of the 500-Acre Law; the establishing of a system of credit for Puerto Rican farmers; the development of local industry; distribution among the landless of land held by sugar companies in excess of five hundred acres; laws to protect wage earners; and a program of slum clearance.

Muñoz Marín and his party were blessed with good luck as well as good intentions. With the outbreak of World War II there suddenly developed a big market in the United States for Puerto Rican rum. Liquor is taxed heavily by the federal government in the United States, and all excise collected there on Puerto Rican rum was returned to the island treasury. This windfall allowed the

Puerto Rican government to increase its annual budget from $22 million in 1938 to $150 million in 1945. So there actually was money in the Puerto Rican till with which to purchase lands in excess of five hundred acres; for the first time, Puerto Rico was not dependent on the U.S. Congress's appropriation of funds to carry out a project that the U.S. Congress was sure to disapprove.

World War II produced some other benefits (at least in the short range) for Puerto Rico as well. The draft took many men from the island and so reduced by that amount the level of unemployment and later added to Puerto Rican total income through veterans' benefits. It is doubtful that many Puerto Ricans relished the army, either for themselves or for their sons, as an economic cure, but in cold statistical terms it did have a positive effect. Too, Puerto Rico's geographical location gave it a tremendous strategic importance from a military point of view, and the United States armed forces spent a great deal of money and provided a large number of jobs in the process of developing naval and military bases. Finally, the war put an end to the depression in the United States. Still linked inextricably to the United States economy, Puerto Rico experienced an easing of economic pressures as the mainland economy moved into full swing.

In 1941 Puerto Rico and the Popular Democratic party had another piece of luck. This came in the form of the appointment of Rexford Guy

Tugwell as Puerto Rico's governor. Tugwell was noteworthy for two reasons: he was the only Anglo-American governor of Puerto Rico of any exceptional merit; and he was the last Anglo-American governor that the island was to have. It was the first of these qualities that was the most important, at least at first, for unlike so many of his predecessors Governor Tugwell became deeply concerned with the problems of the Puerto Rican people and, instead of functioning as an obstacle to efforts of the island legislature to better conditions on the island, he became a useful ally and an effective go-between in Puerto Rico's dealings with the federal government.

Under Muñoz Marín's leadership the Puerto Rican government began to take a positive hand in the direction of the island economy. It purchased from the moribund PRRA the cement plant that had been meant to spark Puerto Rican industrialization, then built a factory for making glass bottles and one for the making of cardboard. A major program of electrification was begun, and Puerto Rico's many streams were harnessed in a hydroelectric system to provide electric power for lighting, home appliances, and powered machinery that improved Puerto Rican production in many different ways. The legislature enacted a measure that allowed the purchase of agricultural lands held in excess of the 500-Acre Law by right of eminent domain, which decreased the time-consuming litigation that had frustrated the PRRA attempts at agrarian reform. Small parcels of land were made available to many landless Puerto Ricans, providing them with home and garden sites. The budget for education was increased and, with people beginning to feel at last that Puerto Rico's destiny was beginning to be shaped by Puerto Rican hands, even the rate of illiteracy began to fall dramatically.

In 1943 Governor Tugwell recommended that the people of Puerto Rico be allowed to elect their own governor, a recommendation that was accepted by President Roosevelt and passed on by the U.S. Congress, though it would be another five years before the recommendation was realized in action.

In 1944 the Popular party won an overwhelming majority in the legislature, ending the political split that had often in the past four years severely hampered legislative efforts. But in that same year a faction of the Popular party became impatient with Muñoz Marín's refusal to work for a final settlement of Puerto Rico's status. What had originally seemed a decision to mute an acknowledged strong sentiment for independence was beginning to seem like avoidance. The dissidents in the Popular party broke away and founded the Pro-Independence Movement under the leadership of Gilberto Concepcíon de Gracia.

In 1946 Governor Tugwell left his post and President Truman appointed Jesus T. Piñero, then Resident Commissioner, to replace him. For the first time in Puerto Rico's history a Puerto Rican occupied the highest government post in the island.

In 1947 the Puerto Rican government took a step of far-reaching consequences in its search for ways to spur the industrial development of the island. A law permitting a tax exemption for industries established on the island by United States companies became the basis a few years later for Puerto Rico's now famous Operation Bootstrap (to be discussed in more detail later), which started a flood of investment capital for the development of tourism, manufacturing, and commerce. World War II had been profitable for many businesses in the United States, and there was a supply of capital in search of profitable investment.

In that same year, the newly formed Independence party took the case of Puerto Rico to the United Nations and asked its help in resolving the political status of Puerto Rico. The principal response to this move came from the U.S. Congress, which decided to let Puerto Rico elect its own governor.

In 1948 the people of Puerto Rico for the first time in the island's post-Columbian history elected their own governor. The man chosen was Luis Muñoz Marín. And now the Popular party finally took a stand on the question of Puerto Rico's status. The best answer for Puerto Rico, Muñoz Marín had decided, lay in autonomy. Muñoz Marín proposed an *Estado Libre Asociado* (Free Associated State) that would provide for local self-government but would preserve relations with the United States. Some called this abandonment of an independence position realistic in the face of United States power; others called it opportunistic. Many, happy to see Puerto Rico's economic life improving as its measure of self-government increased, were also happy to go along with Muñoz Marín and his party.

The Nationalist party called it treason. One evidence of their continued real presence in the Puerto Rican political scene was an almost unanimous student strike at the University of Puerto Rico to protest the university authorities' refusal to allow Albizu Campos to speak on campus.

World opinion against colonialism after World War II, plus the United States claim to leadership of the "free world" in the developing Cold War, made its government sensitive to accusations that it was itself maintaining a colonial relationship with Puerto Rico. Congress faced a problem: how to let Puerto Rico be sovereign and self-governing and at the same time retain the power over it delegated by the Treaty of Paris. The solution arrived at after considerable struggle was contained in Public Law 600, which provided for the oganization of a constitutional government by the people of Puerto Rico. The political status of Puerto Rico under its new government would be that of a Commonwealth translated into Spanish as Free Associated State. In effect, Public Law 600 authorized the people of Puerto Rico to hold a constitutional convention if a plebiscite voted to accept the law and thereby create a government based on the express will of the Puerto Rican people. However, any constitution they might draw up would have to be approved by the U.S. Congress before it could take effect, and it would have to continue the relationship between Puerto Rico and the United States that had been defined by the Jones Act in 1900.

Public Law 600 was signed by President Truman in 1950; June 4, 1951, was set as the date for a special referendum to determine whether or not the people of Puerto Rico would accept their new status.

Nationalists reacted strongly against the proposed constitution which would not alter the basic relationship between the United States and Puerto Rico. Statehood advocates argued against the measure as well, on the grounds that the new form of status was meant to preclude statehood. Action taken by the Nationalists to express their determination to end Puerto Rico's relationship to the United States was both direct and drastic. On October 28, 1950, under Nationalist direction, inmates of the Río Piedras prison mutinied. More than one hundred persons escaped; two guards were killed. On October 30 four Nationalists attacked the governor's mansion in San Juan. In the gun battle that followed, all four Nationalists and one policeman were killed. On the same day a Nationalist group led by a woman, Blanca Canales, attacked and took the police barracks at Jayuya.

Martial law was declared and units of the National Guard defeated the Nationalist revolutionaries. Gun battles with police were also fought by Nationalists in the towns of Utuado, Arecibo, Ponce, and Mayagüez. José Luis Vivas lists the casualties of the October uprising as follows: seven police dead, twenty-one wounded; one National Guardsman dead, eleven wounded; one fireman dead, one wounded; eighteen Nationalists dead, eleven wounded; two bystanders dead, seven wounded. Total: twenty-nine dead, fifty-one wounded.[6]

On November 1, 1950, an attack was made on Blair House in Washington, where President Truman was living, by two Puerto Rican Nationalists, Oscar Collazo and Griselo Torresola. Torresola was killed. Collazo, wounded, was taken into custody. In San Juan the next morning Albizu Campos and the entire Nationalist party leadership were arrested, as were many of the Independence party. Collazo was tried in Washington and sentenced to die August 1, 1952. Later, after President Truman was flooded with letters from other countries, particularly those of Latin America—letters which expressed recognition of the political nature of the Puerto Rican Nationalists' attempt—urging commutation of Collazo's sentence, it was changed to life imprisonment.

In the rash of trials following the October uprisings in Puerto Rico, Albizu Campos was sentenced to seventy-nine years in prison. On September 30, 1953, Governor Muñoz Marín exercised his right of clemency and released him from jail. Accounts in the San Juan press attributed the governor's action to concern for Albizu Campos's bad health and advanced age. There were also speculations that the governor acted to counter claims that the famous revolutionary was being tortured while in prison. Interestingly, Albizu Campos refused his liberty unless other Nationalist prisoners were included. Puerto Rico's Secretary of Justice, however, said:

> Mr. Albizu Campos has no right in the law either to reject or to accept the resolution of pardon issued by the governor. By virtue of that resolution he is a free citizen. The governor granted the pardon because of Albizu Campos's age and state of health. Naturally this has nothing to do with other prisoners sentenced by the courts for crimes that occurred at the same time as those crimes for which he was sentenced.[7]

Meanwhile, on June 4, 1951, the people of Puerto Rico voted to call a Constituent Assembly. Their choice in the referendum was between accepting the United States proposal of Commonwealth status or retaining the system as it then existed. They accepted; and almost at once a controversy arose over what the new status would really mean. For Governor Muñoz Marín the fact that Puerto Rico would draw up its own constitution meant that it could no longer be characterized as a colony of the United States. Members of the United States government, however, were just as insistent that no United States power over the island and the lives of its inhabitants had been lost. According to Joseph Mahoney, chairman of the House Committee on Interior and Insular Affairs: "The U.S. Constitution gives Congress complete control and nothing in the Puerto Rican Constitution could affect or amend or alter that right." [8]

The latter contention seemed borne out in actual congressional response to the constitution that was drafted by the Puerto Rican convention and accepted by the Puerto Rican people in a referendum held on March 3, 1952. The newly drafted Puerto Rican Constitution was then sent to the United States for presidential and congressional approval. After considerable reiteration of the principle that Congress still retained intact the powers granted it by the Treaty of Paris, it refused to approve the Puerto Rican Constitution until the people of Puerto Rico amended it by deleting Article II, Section 20 from the Bill of Rights:

> The Commonwealth also recognizes the existence of the following human rights:
> The right of every person to receive free elementary and secondary education.
> The right of every person to obtain work.
> The right of every person to a standard of living adequate for the health and well-being of himself and of his family, and especially to food, clothing, housing, and medical care and necessary social services.
> The right of every person to social protection in the event of unemployment, sickness, old age, or disability.
> The right of motherhood and childhood to special care and assistance.
> The rights set forth in this section are closely con-

nected with the progressive development of the economy of the Commonwealth and require, for their full effectiveness, sufficient resources and an agricultural and industrial development not yet attained by the Puerto Rican community.

In the light of their duty to achieve the full liberty of the citizen, the people and the government of Puerto Rico shall do everything in their power to promote the greatest possible expansion of the system of production, to assure the fairest distribution of economic output, and to obtain the maximum understanding between individual initiative and collective cooperation. The executive and judicial branches shall bear in mind this duty and shall construe the laws that tend to fulfill it in the most favorable manner possible.

In addition to the deletion of the above, the U.S. Congress insisted on the addition of the following statement to Article VII, Section 3:

Any amendment or revision of this constitution shall be consistent with the resolution enacted by the Congress of the United States approving this constitution, with the applicable provisions of the Constitution of the United States, with the Puerto Rican Federal Relations Act, and with Public Law 600, Eighty-first Congress, adopted in the nature of a compact.[9]

The Puerto Rican Federal Relations Act mentioned above contained the provisions of the Jones Act.

Perhaps symbolically, the Commonwealth Constitution of Puerto Rico was inaugurated on the island on July 25, 1952, the fifty-fourth anniversary of the United States invasion. At a ceremony in

San Juan, Governor Muñoz Marín raised the flag
of Puerto Rico to fly alongside the flag of the United States.

And yet the debate on Puerto Rican status continued, as it still does today. An extensive review of
the controversy from the adoption of the Commonwealth Constitution until today is not possible
here, but even a few brief highlights are revealing.

March 1953: The United States announced that
it would no longer report to the United Nations as
to the social, economic, and educational conditions
in Puerto Rico as it had been required to do on the
grounds that Puerto Rico was not self-governing.
After bitter debate in the UN, and after some arm-
twisting of representatives by the United States
delegation, the UN upheld the United States position by a narrow vote.

March 1954: Four Puerto Rican Nationalists entered the United States House of Representatives
and opened fire on the congressmen present. Five
congressmen were wounded; seventeen Puerto
Ricans were indicted and tried on charges of conspiracy; thirteen were found guilty.

1958: Admission of Alaska (and a little later
Hawaii) to statehood revived the hopes of the pro-
statehood faction in Puerto Rico. Obviously, Puerto Rico's geography and nonwhite ethnic elements
could no longer provide arguments of force
against their admission to the Union.

1963: Because of the continuing debate over
Puerto Rico's political status, and tacitly recognizing that its Commonwealth status had been de-

fined as a temporary expedient, the governments of the United States and Puerto Rico agreed to establish a United States – Puerto Rico Commission on the Status of Puerto Rico to study the question and to report on possible alternatives for a permanent solution.

1966: The Commission reported that there were three possible alternatives for Puerto Rican status – Commonwealth, statehood, or independence – and indicated its belief that choice among the three should be left to the Puerto Rican people.

1967: Puerto Rico ordered an island plebiscite to determine the will of the Puerto Rican people as to the status issue. The choices offered were statehood, independence, and the continuation of Commonwealth status. But the plebiscite had no binding force on the U.S. Congress. If its results favored statehood, it would still be up to the U.S. Congress to decide whether and when statehood might be granted. The same would be true if the vote were for independence. Even to make Commonwealth a clearly permanent status would require action by the U.S. Congress.

In the plebiscite, Commonwealth received the most votes, but the controversy continued. The Independence party boycotted the plebiscite. Afterward, its partisans claimed that abstentions were really votes for independence; adding to those the votes that were cast for independence in spite of the party boycott, independence advocates claimed that, in fact, the majority of Puerto Rico's voters expressed a preference for independence.

Both statehood advocates and Commonwealth supporters agreed that the small number of votes actually cast for independence showed that Puerto Ricans wanted to continue their connection with the United States. Statehood advocates, however, claimed that Muñoz Marín, who campaigned heavily in favor of Commonwealth, not only took advantage of his personal popularity but also misrepresented the meaning of Commonwealth to the voters. Commonwealth supporters, of course, accepted the plebiscite vote as conclusive evidence of their support by the Puerto Rican people.

1968: In the election for the governorship of Puerto Rico, the millionaire industrialist Luis A. Ferré won the contest. (But not against Muñoz Marín: age had forced his retirement from public life.) With Ferré's election, even the contested meaning of the 1967 plebiscite was weakened, for Ferré was openly an advocate of statehood. After his election, Ferré claimed that by voting for him the Puerto Rican people had repealed the results of the 1967 plebiscite.

The status of Puerto Rico has yet to be resolved. Today there is still a large body of opinion in the U.S. Congress that Puerto Rico is whatever the United States permits it to be. Even under its own constitution it does not yet have as broad an acceptance from the United States of its right to shape its own destiny as was expressed by Spain in the Autonomous Charter of 1898.

8

AMERICANIZATION

Since the end of World War II, and especially since the establishment of the Commonwealth, Puerto Ricans have been in control of their own affairs — at least within the limits and limitations imposed on the island's people by the United States and the Federal Relations Act. Something of the political struggle through which Puerto Ricans achieved the degree of self-government that they now have has been described; the changes they have brought about in their island as a consequence have been dramatic. Just a few samples may serve to give an idea of the tremendous alteration in the conditions of life for Puerto Rico's people in physical and material terms in the last thirty years since the governments they have elected have been able to mobilize the island's resources.

In 1940, as has been stated, the life expectancy of a Puerto Rican was forty-six years; today it is

seventy years, which is as high as for the United
States, and mortality rates are among the lowest in
the world. Per capita income was $118 per year in
1940; in 1969 it was $1,234. Industry earns four
times as much each year as agriculture does, destroying the centuries-old image of Puerto Rico as
a rural society dependent entirely on the produce
of its sugar-cane fields, its tobacco rows, and its
coffee plantations. In the number of its television
sets, automobiles, telephones, refrigerators, and
radios per thousand inhabitants, Puerto Rico
ranks high among modern societies.

The changes made in Puerto Rico since its
achievement of a real measure of self-government
are reflected not only in lists of statistics but in the
daily way of life of its people. While it is impossible
to describe how a "typical" Puerto Rican individual
or family lives, there are ways in which Puerto
Rico's growth can be seen to affect the majority of
Puerto Rican lives. For example, whether in a city,
town, or rural hamlet, most Puerto Rican families
today have electricity and safe drinking water.
Their children have access to schools; education at
least through high school is a practical hope for
the children of most Puerto Rican families. Medical care, which once was the prerogative of the
wealthy, is available to the majority of Puerto Rican people, though — as in the United States — the
quality and quantity of medical attention available
to any person varies in proportion to his or her
ability to pay for it.

Puerto Rico's increased industrialization has

provided many jobs that simply did not exist before the 1940s. This has drawn an increasingly large number of Puerto Ricans into the island's principal cities. Coupled with the heavy pressures against the small landowner from the giant land corporations (mostly United States owned) the attraction of city jobs has spurred such an urban migration that it is no longer possible to think of Puerto Rico as principally rural. More and more, the jobs are in the cities. And most Puerto Ricans work for somebody else. Many work in the plants and factories that produce goods for sale in the United States; many work in the hotels, clubs, etc., that accommodate the mainland tourists. Nevertheless, many do own and operate small businesses of their own: shops, repair services, and so forth.

Nowadays, for most urban Puerto Ricans at least, life is similar in many ways to that of their mainland contemporaries. The work of a Puerto Rican mechanic, bookkeeper, or schoolteacher is similar to that of a mechanic, bookkeeper, or schoolteacher in Ohio. The material goals and comforts, even the "civilized" amenities and entertainments such as movies, television, automobiles, checking accounts, and frozen dinners that are a part of living in Ohio are also commonplaces for many Puerto Ricans. One big difference, however, is that almost invariably the Puerto Rican employee receives a lower wage for the same work than his or her mainland counterpart. And the Puerto Rican consumer must pay more for the same goods that the mainland dweller buys for less. Coupled with the still relatively low opportunities for employment, the still relatively high inadequacy in decent housing, and the relatively high lack of technical education, the majority of Puerto Rican people must struggle much harder to attain the standard of living considered normal in Ohio, though they are under the same pressures from advertising and the public media to identify the "good life" in much the same terms as on the mainland.

There is one advantage that Puerto Rico enjoys which must be mentioned, even at the risk of appearing to digress. As has already been pointed out, Puerto Rico's ethnic roots are in America, Europe, and Africa—as are those of the United States. In Puerto Rico, however, integration is a reality. It is not true that there is no consciousness of color in Puerto Rico, nor that there are no relative values attached socially to color. But compared with the United States prejudice and racism are virtually absent. There is no real stigma attached to racial intermarriage, nor is any real discrimination in employment or education practiced against Black people, unless it is by a mainland employer who learned his attitudes in the United States. In Puerto Rico *Negra* ("Black Girl") is a term of endearment among all classes and may be applied to a woman friend whether her appearance is African or Nordic. Racial acceptance on a social level, however, does thin out radically among the Puerto Rican social aristocracy, among whom *sangre pura* (pure blood) is highly valued. Though such an aristocrat, usually of Spanish descent, will accept a Black person without question as a business or political colleague, that same Black person is excluded from his more intimate social life.

It would appear that Muñoz Marín's appeal to Puerto Ricans to support a government that would make the issue of political status secondary to the solving of their material and physical problems was based on very sound reasoning, and that it has borne good fruit. But the Puerto Rican people have not ceased to be concerned with the question of their political status in relation to the United States. The division between statehood aspirants and independence aspirants remains. In fact, in recent years it has grown sharper. Perhaps because neither has seemed immediately attainable, partisans of each have often supported the Commonwealth at least tacitly and tried to interpret it as a logical step toward their own goal. There are many, of course, who would like Commonwealth to *be* the final solution to the status issue; but the refusal of the United States to allow the people of Puerto Rico to define *any* status for themselves as final (Congress has not yet given up the right it claims to do that for them) keeps alive the consciousness that even the Commonwealth government that has existed in fact for nearly twenty years may be only temporary. For that matter, it is impossible to tell how many of those who have supported the Commonwealth idea on those occasions that they have been asked to express an opinion have done so as a choice between the lesser of two evils, rather than because Commonwealth fulfills their real aspirations. No one knows, which is precisely one of the factors that keeps the question of status agitated.

For the people and politicians of the United States, it appears to be very easy to misinterpret the Puerto Rican division between pro-independence and pro-statehood sentiment. "Statehood advocates," mainland citizens seem to say, "must like us. Independence advocates are anti-American." What Puerto Ricans express, however, is something different. They are concerned with themselves, with the kind of cultural identity they want Puerto Ricans to possess and reflect. Puerto Ricans may like "Americans" and yet not want to *be* "Americans." The division between pro-independence and pro-statehood sentiment seems to be, at its root, a cultural one. Ismael Rodríguez Bou described the split in referring to the issue of whether English or Spanish should be the language used to teach Puerto Rican children in public schools. "Those in favor of English as the language of instruction were identified as American *asimilistas* [assimilationists], and those in favor of Spanish as *separatistas* [separationists]. To this day the teaching of English has never been able to free itself from a certain political involvement."[1]

Nor has almost any other manifestation of Americanization, and the reasons are not hard to see. From the very beginning of the United States occupation it was assumed and stated by United States authorities that Puerto Ricans must be Americanized before they could participate fully in the United States system. Some Puerto Ricans agreed, or at least were willing to accede in return for full participation. Others preferred to be Puerto Ricans. But the United States held political control, and the United States has not yet made up its mind either to accept Puerto Ricans as full participants, or to exclude them. In the face of the United States preference for keeping them in a sort of halfway house (which some people call colonialism), Puerto Ricans of both persuasions have struggled to take political power into their own hands: the one, to achieve full participation; the other, to achieve emancipation. But willy-nilly, since the relationship between Puerto Rico and the United States has continued to be a fact, the pressures exerted by the latter to reshape the former in its own image have continued. Those pressures are many and constant, and Puerto Ricans' continued experience of them does much to keep alive their concern about political status.

One of the areas in which this cultural conflict has been the most obvious — and has had very real consequences — is in that of education. For the light that consideration of Puerto Rico's problems with education since the United States invasion can shed on both sides of the culture conflict, it seems worth reviewing at least briefly from the beginning.

From 1900 to 1952 education in Puerto Rico was under the authority of Commissioners of Education appointed by the president of the United States. Until 1930 those commissioners were always Anglo-Americans. They had explicit directions to work for the Americanization of Puerto Rico and, most specifically, to turn them into an English-speaking people. Some of the early advice from Anglo-American educators betrayed a startling ignorance of Puerto Rico and its people. For example, Dr. Victor S. Clark, who was in charge of education under the military government of 1899, stated:

> There does not seem to be among the masses the same devotion to their native tongue or to any national ideal that animates the Frenchman, for instance, in Canada or the Rhine provinces. Another important fact that must not be overlooked, is that a majority of the people of this island does not speak pure Spanish. Their language is a patois almost unintelligible to the natives of Barcelona and Madrid. It possesses no literature and little value as an intellectual medium. There is a bare possibility that it will be nearly as easy to educate this people out of their patois into English as it will be to educate them into the elegant tongue of Castile.[2]

Dr. Pedro A. Cebollero discusses Dr. Clark's statement in "A School Language Policy for Puerto Rico," as follows:

In making such a hasty generalization about the quality of the Spanish spoken by the Puerto Ricans, Dr. Clark was unaware that the Castilian form of Spanish is not spoken in Spain itself outside the province of Castile and that the difference between Castilian and Spanish as spoken in most of Spain and in the Spanish countries of America is a matter of the pronunciation of a few letters and of a certain rhythm and inflection. His reference to Barcelona as a place where the Puerto Rican brand of Spanish would not be understood is particularly unfortunate because the native of Barcelona does not speak Spanish but Catalán, one of the principal dialects of Spain. That the Spanish spoken in Puerto Rico is as good as that spoken in most of Spain and better than the Spanish spoken in many provinces of Spain itself has been attested by Dr. Tomás Navarro Tomás, a noted Spanish philologist from the University of Madrid, who recently made a study of spoken Spanish in Puerto Rico.[3]

Just on the question of the use of English in Puerto Rico's schools Dr. Rodríguez Bou has noted seven different phases since the United States invasion.

1. *1899-1900*: English was established as the only language in which classes could be taught in Puerto Rican schools.

2. *1900-1905*: Spanish was used as the classroom language in the elementary grades; English was used in the secondary grades.

3. *1905-1916*: English was the only language used in Puerto Rican classrooms.

4. *1916-1934*: Spanish was the classroom lan-

guage of grades 1-4; grade 5 was taught half in Spanish and half in English; from grade 6 on all classes were taught in English.

This system was studied by the International Institute of Teachers College of Columbia University as early as 1925. Of that study's findings Dr. Rodríguez says that it

> . . . found that the achievement of students in English at the end of the third grade did not justify the effort, the time, and the money devoted to its teaching, and that even less justified was the denial of opportunities to the rest of the subjects in the curriculum. The study made by the institute recommended that English be taught from the fourth grade on instead of beginning its teaching in the first grade. However, the sensible recommendations made on the basis of the findings of the Teachers College survey were disregarded, and until 1934 the English language continued to be taught from the first grade.[4]

5. *1916-1936*: The first Puerto Rican Commissioner of Education, Dr. José Padín, carried out his own study of the previous system and found that it didn't work very well. After eight years' schooling, students did not adequately learn to speak, understand, read, or write in English. And since most of the subjects that they studied were taught in English it is doubtful that they learned much science, history, or mathematics either. Dr. Padín, more interested in instruction than in Americanization, changed the system. Spanish be-

came the classroom language in the elementary grades, with English taught as a second language. Still, teaching English took up a double period each day, and English continued to be the classroom language in the secondary grades.

6. *1937-1949*: President Franklin D. Roosevelt and his Secretary of the Interior, Harold L. Ickes, expressed personal concern over the failure of previous commissioners to turn Puerto Ricans into an English-speaking people. In a letter to Dr. José M. Gallardo, his appointee to the post of Commissioner of Education, President Roosevelt wrote:

I desire at this time to make clear the attitude of my administration on the extremely important matter of teaching English in Puerto Rico. Puerto Rico came under the American flag thirty-eight years ago. Nearly twenty years ago Congress extended American citizenship to Puerto Ricans. It is regrettable that today, hundreds of thousands of Puerto Ricans have little and often virtually no knowledge of the English language. Moreover, even among those who have had the opportunity to study English in the public schools, mastery of the language is far from satisfactory. It is an indispensable part of American policy that the coming generation of American citizens in Puerto Rico grow up with complete facility in the English tongue. It is the language of our Nation. Only through the acquisition of this language will Puerto Rican Americans secure a better understanding of American ideals and principles. Moreover, it is only through familiarity with our language that the Puerto Ricans will be able to take full advantage of the economic opportunities which became available to them when they were made American citizens.[5]

Dr. Gallardo, spurred by this message, abandoned the Padín policy and experimented with different methods. But by 1942 the results of his own experiments led him to establish Spanish as the classroom language for the first six grades, with both English and Spanish used in the secondary grades. He was supported in his conclusions by Dr. Algernon Coleman, professor of French at the University of Chicago and a member of the Committee on Modern Languages of the American Council on Education. Dr. Coleman had visited Puerto Rico in 1939 and, after studying the school system there, had been concerned enough with what he saw to write directly to Secretary Ickes, to challenge the United States policies with regard to Puerto Rican education. After pointing out the damage done by making a school system subject to arbitrary decisions made by political appointees subject to political pressures, Dr. Coleman discussed some of the specific problems.

> There has been much talk of an educational program whereby the children of the Island ought to be made really bilingual. Such a purpose seems wholly unreal to one who is ever so little expert in these matters. We know, for example, what has been the outcome of the long-time effort of the British to accomplish this in India. Spanish will continue to be the mother tongue of all Puerto Ricans. . . . Few of our theorists on the subject seem to realize the small number of opportunities that most Puerto Ricans have for speaking English in any continuous fashion as a genuine vehicle of intercourse with others. . . .
>
> It seems to me that too little attention has been given

to formulating and applying useful criteria for choosing textbooks in most Puerto Rican schools. It is fallacious to assume that the same criteria may be applied in selecting textbooks for children in Massachusetts, Illinois, Georgia, and Puerto Rico. The experiential background, the intellectual background, the vernacular background of the island group must be taken into account. I do not mean that children in the Island should see books based only on the flora, the fauna, the traditions, the customs, the history of their own territory. At present, however, the current sets quite the other way, and the textbooks in use are almost wholly foreign to the background in which the young islanders live. For example, I observed high-school classes in which, following the textbook, the teachers were laying stress on the avoidance of linguistic errors common among the English-speaking people on the continent. Such language lessons are of small use in correcting the errors prevalent among Spanish-speaking people when using English. . . .

The teaching of English has for the last forty years absorbed most of the financial resources of the school system of Puerto Rico. Those of us who are interested in the problem should be able to look in that direction for light. We find none: and with all due respect, Mr. Secretary, I insist that your Department is not properly discharging its duty to the island in regard to the teaching of English.[6]

Whatever effect Dr. Coleman's letter may have had on Secretary Ickes it did not prevent him from taking Dr. Gallardo so severely to task for his decision to use Spanish as the classroom language that Dr. Gallardo felt compelled to resign his post. He resumed it, however, on Secretary Ickes's invi-

tation. But from that time until 1949, the issue of
Spanish vs. English continued to involve Puerto
Rican educators and United States policy makers
in controversy and to divide *separatistas* from *asimilistas*.

7. *1949-*   : Professor Mariano Villaronga was
appointed commissioner by the first elected governor of Puerto Rico, Luis Muñoz Marín. Commissioner Villaronga declared the following was
his policy for all public schools in Puerto Rico:
". . . Spanish will be the vehicle of instruction in
the high-school. This change, which responds to a
long-felt need, extends definitely the use of the
vernacular as the teaching means until the last
year of high school."

The rule that Spanish should be the classroom
language in all grades applied only to public
schools. Private schools continued to do as they
pleased about language. Then, in 1962, an effort
was made to get private Catholic schools to ob-
serve the language rule. What happened is a practical example of the way that the United States
continues to exercise control over even purely cultural matters in Puerto Rico in spite of Commonwealth and its Constitution.

In 1962 there were nearly sixty thousand students enrolled in private schools, and about half of
them received all or part of their classroom instruction in English. Most of the private schools
were Catholic, directed by Anglo-American nuns,
and leaned heavily toward Americanization of

their students, among whom the economically and socially lower classes were scarcely represented. That year, a group of concerned parents of private school children addressed a public letter to the bishops of Puerto Rico (all of whom were Anglo-Americans), asking that their children be taught in Spanish. Their cause was taken up by the Bishop Arizmendi Society for the Defense of the Language, and soon considerable public furor, pro and con, was being raised. The Secretary of Public Instruction, Cándido Oliveras, took a stand on the issue and declared himself in favor of Spanish as the classroom language, saying that he believed he had the authority to refuse accreditation to any school which, without very good reason, failed to teach in Spanish. At this point several United States congressmen made public statements opposing the position taken by the Puerto Rican secretary. Representative Adam Clayton Powell, chairman of the House Committee on Education, warned that Puerto Rico might lose the federal funds that it received in aid for public schools if Secretary Cándido Oliveras's views were put into effect and Spanish were required in the private schools. Governor Muñoz Marín was first reported in a newspaper interview as supporting the secretary's position, but only a few days later said that the Puerto Rican government would not interfere in the private schools.

The private schools continue to use English as the classroom language.

The concern that Dr. Coleman expressed in his letter to Secretary Ickes as to the quality of textbooks used in Puerto Rico's public schools has been repeated again and again by Puerto Ricans concerned with the education of their children and with the preservation of Puerto Rican cultural identity. Even non-Puerto Ricans have challenged the relevancy of textbooks used in Puerto Rico's public schools. A report made by the Institute of Field Studies of Teachers College, Columbia University, in 1948-49, said in part:

> Puerto Rican children spend much time reading about little boys and girls in the United States riding tricycles, playing in boats, and having luxurious doll houses in spacious playrooms. At the only time during which thousands of the children will have an opportunity to learn how to live better lives in Puerto Rico, they are spending long hours of each school year reading about haystacks, steam shovels, skating on the ice, and sliding down hills in snow.
>
> In the urban junior and senior high schools . . . youth have printed materials in social studies which deal only with the history and government of the United States and with the trends in world government. The pupil reads materials dealing with the colonists' arrival in North America, the establishment of the new country, the rivalry between the North and the South, and the emergence of the United States as a world power. Because of the relationship existing between Puerto Rico and the United States, and because of the importance today of world understanding, materials dealing with the government and history of the Continent should be available to these children, it is true.

However, it is unrealistic to expect an educational program to meet the needs and abilities of children in
Puerto Rico unless most of the materials deal with the
development of Puerto Rico, its culture, its government, its socio-economic problems, its relationship with
the United States, and its role among Latin American
nations.[7]

Though written in 1949, the report quoted from
is still relevant to the situation in Puerto Rico today.

There are other channels than education
through which pressures to Americanize have
been exerted on the Puerto Rican people — or perhaps it is more accurate to say that there are ways
to educate other than the formal school system.
For example, the United States insistence on the
separation of Church and State removed Catholic
influence from public schools and took public
funds away from the Catholic Church. A flood of
Protestant missionaries came to the island. The
social work performed by these groups has been
considerable. So has the Americanization, for the
line is often blurred between religious dogma and
the cultural habits of the Anglo-American religious teachers.

The United States military services have also
created pressures for Americanization on the
Puerto Rican people, both by their presence on
the island and through their effect on Puerto Ricans who have put on United States uniforms.
During World War I, about 18,000 Puerto Rican

men served with the United States Army; in World War II more than 65,000; and during the Korean War more than 43,000. From the time the Universal Military Training and Service Act went into effect until 1963 almost 89,000 Puerto Ricans have been drafted, and thousands more during the long years of the United States intervention in Vietnam. This represents an Americanization force with a vengeance, for army attitudes are narrow and army discipline is strict. In addition, there are those who have chosen to make a career of military service and so their wives and children may spend years on or about military posts in the United States or abroad.

The United States military presence is strongly felt in Puerto Rico, where army, air force, and navy bases occupy a large part of the 13 percent of Puerto Rico's tillable land still controlled by the federal government. An ordinary Shell Oil road map identifies seventeen different military installations, and it is said that large areas of lands described officially as National Park are in fact used to train soldiers for Vietnam-style warfare. More than half of the island of Vieques is held as a naval reservation, while most of the island of Culebra is used by the navy as a target area for ship-to-shore shelling. This use of Culebra, and the consequent wounding of several of its Puerto Rican inhabitants, sparked militant protests by Puerto Rican students in 1971.

The wars that the United States has taken part

in since it acquired Puerto Rico have had their effect on the island population as well. During the two World Wars, Puerto Rico's civilian population was involved in bond selling, etc., and were subjected to all the influences that the United States government could muster to keep up the morale and patriotic fervor of its citizens, including the official condolences for the survivors of those killed; pensions for those maimed; and veterans' benefits for those unhurt. Through their being involved in United States wars, Puerto Ricans have learned one more facet of "the American way of life."

The long years during which Puerto Rico was ruled by Anglo-American governors; when its most important governmental and administrative posts were filled by Anglo-American appointees; when Puerto Rican economic and legal and cultural institutions were being reshaped in ways more to the liking of the United States: the effects of those years on the Puerto Rican psychology, and particularly on that of children growing up without the memory of any other conditions, is not difficult to imagine. And the resulting potential for negative reaction — for anti-Americanization, so to speak — should be also apparent.

But the most massive forces working to destroy Puerto Rican culture and Puerto Rican identity are the ones that have accompanied the economic changes made on the island since the creation of the Commonwealth and the launching of Opera-

tion Bootstrap. Much glittering rhetoric has surrounded Operation Bootstrap since its beginnings
in the early 1950s; it has been praised in popular
writings, dissected in learned essays, and interpret-
ed in political studies to the point that it seems
superfluous to discuss it at great length here.
Briefly, however, Operation Bootstrap represented an effort by the Puerto Rican government to
harness the abilities and energies of its people to
create the necessary mechanisms of a healthy society within the limitations on economic freedom
imposed on the island by the United States. On
the one hand this meant providing social services,
such as education, health care, drinkable water,
and so forth; and public services, such as roads,
electricity, transportation, etc., to the masses of the
Puerto Rican people. It meant creating a job market for Puerto Rico's unemployed so that they
could work and earn and provide for their own
needs. On the other hand, it meant finding a way
to pay for the schools and hospitals and roads; it
meant finding the capital needed to build the factories and to set up the commercial enterprises
that would provide the jobs. And it meant doing
so without antagonizing the United States government and United States business lobbies, for the
Puerto Rican experiences of the 1930s and 1940s
had demonstrated how difficult the United States
could make it for any system to prosper in Puerto
Rico if it stepped on the toes of United States economic interests or showed signs of functioning in

some "socialist" way that competed with or inhibited "free enterprise."

To answer this challenge, the Commonwealth government took advantage of the tax-exemption laws passed in 1947 to stimulate foreign investment and revised them as part of a concerted drive to attract manufacturing and commercial capital from the United States. It offered tax exemption for periods ranging from ten to seventeen years; it sometimes built and leased at low rents the physical plants required by new businesses; it functioned as an arbiter between Puerto Rican labor and the new industries to establish minimum-wage rates that would be as attractive as possible to Anglo-American investors.

Much of Operation Bootstrap's efforts went into developing the tourist industry. In addition to advertising heavily the natural attractions of Puerto Rico's tropical beaches and extending the same incentives to hotel operators as to other investors, the government built the island's first big luxury hotel in San Juan and leased it to the Hilton chain. The Cuban revolution a few years later, which resulted in the closing of Havana to many tourists who had been in the habit of going there for their sin and sun, increased the potential tourist trade for San Juan considerably.

United States investors responded with some eagerness to the opportunities for profit that the Commonwealth planners put before them so persuasively, and the 1950s and 1960s saw a tremendous influx of business enterprises. By 1970 there were more than 2,700 manufacturing plants in Puerto Rico, employing 137,000 workers. The Condado section of San Juan had become a glittering Miami Beach type strip of beachfront hotels, providing several thousand rooms for visitors and thousands of jobs for Puerto Ricans. Nightclubs and hotel gambling casinos were added to the attractions of warm beaches and of colonial old San Juan. Tourism had become a $230 million business; the island's gross national product had risen to more than $4 billion.

(There was a debit side to the ledger, too, which revealed two facts of the Puerto Rican economy: first, that the lack of jobs, combined with the increase in population, required still more new jobs than were being created; and, second, that Puerto Rico's increased earnings were not finding their way proportionately to the island's various economic classes, at least not as direct income. Public works, public health, and public education programs benefited urban and rural poor directly. Nevertheless, although the businesses established under the government incentive program made, on the average, significantly higher profits than their mainland counterparts, wages in Puerto Rico remained significantly lower. The average wage in manufacturing was sixty-three dollars per week, while the ratio of dependent Puerto Ricans—that is, persons whose youth or old age placed them outside the labor force—was 3.3 compared to 1.7

in the United States. Unemployment still was in excess of 10 percent; four families in ten were below the two-thousand-dollar "extreme poverty" level; and between 1953 and 1963 the share of Puerto Rico's income received by the poorest one-fifth of the population decreased from 5 percent to 4 percent, which suggests that the very poor were actually becoming poorer while the overall average income was increasing.

A consequence of the tax-exemption incentive for new businesses, furthermore, was to force the burden of supporting Puerto Rico's public programs primarily on wage earners, since the industries and businesses which were their employers were largely exempt. In 1969, according to Kal Wagenheim's *Puerto Rico: A Profile*, not one of the island's seven principal banks paid a penny in income taxes.)[8]

Even admitting the continuing problems in the Puerto Rican economy, however, it cannot be denied that its growth has been impressive. But the pressures it has brought to bear against the Puerto Rican culture are extreme as well. For more and more Puerto Ricans work for "stateside" firms that not only are owned by corporations outside of Puerto Rico but are operated according to Anglo-American values, often at odds with those of the Puerto Rican and Spanish tradition. They produce goods whose primary market is in the United States, and this is so not because there is a United States market for specifically Puerto Rican goods, or even goods made from specifically Puerto Rican materials (which could reinforce Puerto Rican pride in its own identity), but because Puerto Rico is a convenient place for converting raw materials brought to the island into goods that mainland citizens of the United States will buy. The consumer goods flooding the island are, at the same time, essentially those of the United States. They are sold in Puerto Rico in chains of supermarkets such as Grand Union, or in such stores as Walgreen's, J. C. Penney, Franklin's, and Woolworth, all United States owned. Streets and highways are filled with Fords and Chevrolets; kitchens in the cities are filled with appliances from Sunbeam, Westinghouse, and General Electric; the police ride Harley-Davidson motorcycles and carry Smith & Wesson revolvers; supermarket patrons buy canned Del Monte pineapple and frozen Minute Maid orange juice; students cross the street from their schools to get a MacDonald's hamburger for lunch. In 1969 nearly 78 percent of the more than $2 billion that Puerto Ricans spent on imports went to the United States (making Puerto Rico the second biggest customer of the United States in the hemisphere); on the island, almost anything a person might want to own comes bearing an American name.

The effect of mass media such as radio, TV, and motion pictures is hard to calculate but cannot be ignored. More than one million radios receive broadcasts from sixty-seven transmitting stations.

Popular music and news broadcasts are radio staples; United States rock and roll recording stars are as much a part of Puerto Rican radio as they are of Michigan's, and the bulk of news broadcasts come from Associated Press and United Press International wire services. Kal Wagenheim describes a broadcasting day for Puerto Rico's 450,000 TV sets:

A typical morning's fare will include the U.S. weekly drama series *The Millionaire* (dubbed in Spanish), a *"novela"* (soap opera), or a melodramatic Mexican film, which features plenty of shooting, guitar-strumming, tears, and soulful stares. Noontime is "live," as local *comediantes* take over with variety shows that mix music, many commercials, and topical humor, often bordering on the risqué. (Some of the skits satirizing the Jacqueline Kennedy–Aristotle Onassis honeymoon, for example, would have gotten no closer to a U.S. network than the corner burlesque theatre.)

Late afternoon shows, aimed at schoolchildren, offer cartoons, Laurel and Hardy, and the "Three Stooges," who are known here as *"Los Tres Chiflados."* The top-rated "kiddies" show is live and stars an elfin Spaniard named Pacheco who wears a straw hat, bow tie, and doleful countenance. Between cartoons and commercials for toys and cereals, Pacheco reads notes from parents, such as: "My Emilio isn't eating his dinner." Gently, but firmly, he stares into the camera and tells Emilio to eat. Pacheco also warns that his helper, the *parajito investigador* ("the little snooper bird") will be around to check on him. The tactic often improves Emilio's appetite for weeks.

As suppertime approaches, Tarzan battles wild African tribesmen who speak broken Spanish, and also competes with Spiderman, Batman, Jim Bowie and the Flintstones.

The evening offers *Mod Squad, Gunsmoke, The Dean Martin Show* (in English on Channel 18), *I Love Lucy, Perry Mason,* and local musical variety programs. The night ends with the late movie starting about 11 P.M., although English-speaking insomniacs may switch over to Channel 18 to watch a week-old *Johnny Carson Show* tape, which lasts until 1 A.M.

With the exception of the lengthy supper hour news show on Channel 6, television news shows offer only tidbits of world events. Films of the bloody Vietnam conflict, for example, which have caused such an impact on the U.S. mainland, rarely appear on island television.[9]

A marked contrast to the commercial TV stations is the government-operated, low-budget educational station. During the day, it is used as a TV teaching aid and its programs are piped into public schools. In the evenings it broadcasts the works of local writers, or presents documentaries produced by the mainland National Education Television. The latter are usually of excellent quality but are, unfortunately, broadcast in English, which limits their usefulness and appeal.

The more prestigious United States newspapers are flown in daily to Puerto Rico. *El Mundo* is the Puerto Rican daily with the largest circulation and it is controlled by the Knight Newspaper chain. The second largest newspaper, *El Imparcial,* is owned by a former head of the pro-statehood Republican party, while the third largest, *El Día*, belongs to the family of Puerto Rico's Governor Ferré. Opposing all of these politically is *Claridad*, the weekly organ of the *Movimiento Pro Independencia*. An expression of the concern felt in Puerto Rico about this cultural bombardment which has made the "culture conflict" a most unequal contest has been made by Dr. Bou:

> When this clash of cultures took place earlier in the insularism we lived in, when we lacked outside contacts, quick communication, English radio and television programs, English newspapers, magazines, phonograph records, motion pictures, and books (except for the few who could afford such luxuries) the clash of cultures could have continued to "the millennium" without the Puerto Ricans losing much ground. But when all the above-mentioned forces of one of the cultures not only exist but are further strengthened by the economic ramifications of the industries, movies, radio, and television stations, chain stores, the movement of hundreds of thousands of tourists, dozens of night clubs whose shows are mostly in English, buy thousands of English records (Beatles and all), the imitation of teenage rhythms and dances, garments, costumes, symbols, and behavior about which all the means of communication give account, the struggle begins to be one of gradual but sure weakening of the Puerto Rican culture.[10]

Finally, no account of the forces at work to Americanize the Puerto Rican culture can be complete without taking into account the effects of the large migration of Puerto Ricans to the United

States in search of work opportunities. Today
nearly one quarter of Puerto Ricans live in the
United States, where naturally all the pressures
described above are multiplied. There are special
problems that mainland-dwelling Puerto Ricans
face which will be dealt with in some detail in the
next chapter; here it will be enough to point out
the tremendous effect on the "culture conflict"
that must follow the impact on such a large part of
Puerto Rico's people (though it will be seen that
real assimilation is a different matter) moving into
an alien culture.

The question of cultural identity lies close to the
heart of the conflict between independence and
statehood—from the Puerto Rican point of view.
So much so, that although the positive aspects of
independence, such as national pride, the dignity
of standing before the world family of nations as
an equal, are prominent goals in pro-independence argument, it often seems that the fear of
what statehood might do to Puerto Rican cultural
identity is a stronger motivation. In other words,
the demand for independence is often a rejection
of statehood and the cultural destruction seen as
its consequence.

In his presentation to the United States–Puerto
Rico Commission on the Status of Puerto Rico, titled "The Cultural Personality of Puerto Rico and
the Political Status," Eladio Rodríguez Otero de-
velops the *separatista* point of view that statehood
would destroy Puerto Rico's national identity in

short order, while the present Commonwealth system will destroy it as surely, though more slowly.

Were Puerto Rico to become a state, Rodríguez argues, it would represent such a distinct minority among the states that it could not survive the difference. In spite of a legal equality, the pressure of an incompatible and much greater cultural force would destroy that of Puerto Rico. Further, with statehood granted, Puerto Rico would attract many more than the sixty-five thousand or so Anglo-Americans now living on the island and with their already existent economic leverage they would soon dominate the new state on its own soil.

Rodríguez describes the assaults already experienced in Puerto Rico against the Spanish language in spite of the legal equality there of both Spanish and English. If Puerto Rico should become a state, Spanish would be without protection — for obviously, the United States would not accept the legal equality of Spanish in the nation.

> The truth is, gentlemen, that it does not matter that a dozen of North American intellectuals and a few congressmen wish for and say that they favor a certain degree of "cultural pluralism" in the event that Puerto Rico joins as a state among the United States, for really it is not a matter of ideals or of the good intentions of a handful of leaders; it is a matter of what would happen to Puerto Rico, as a matter of reality, as a matter of fact, if it joined the North American Union as a state.[11]

Rodríguez cites a pro-statehood argument

which maintains that the cultural roots of Puerto
Rico are too strong to be absorbed into another
culture unless its population were to be totally dis-
persed, and says in reply:

> But it turns out that history shows exactly the oppo-
> site. New Mexico, California, and Texas are witnesses
> to the tragedy of the great Hispanic nuclei who have
> had the experience of statehood. The Anglo-Ameri-
> cans used the whole force of the law to defeat the cul-
> ture of the people of those states. By means of state
> legislation, both constitutional and ordinary, the En-
> glish language was imposed in the legislatures, in the
> courts and in the schools, both public and private. And
> in the case of Louisiana, the Enabling Act that admitted
> that territory into the Union required as a prerequisite
> that the English language be exclusively used in all
> branches of the government.
>   New Mexico is the state that best illustrates the pro-
> cess of cultural assimilation of one people when another
> gains an economic and industrial advantage that is
> greatly superior. Fifty years after it joined the Union
> the Anglo-Americans, in spite of the fact that they only
> make up half of the population, dominate commerce,
> the banks, industry, politics, the professions, the reli-
> gious institutions, education, and the civic organizations.
> Doctor Joaquín Ortega, of the School of Interamerican
> Affairs at the University of New Mexico, expresses elo-
> quently the tragedy of the Hispanic people of that ter-
> ritory when he says that "New Mexico *still* has usable
> cultural remnants." We ask: Of what worth has legal
> equality been to the New Mexicans of Hispanic culture
> in the state of New Mexico within the Union?
>   The history of the assimilation of New Mexico is a
> history of prejudice, of discrimination, of usurpation,

of assault, of oppression: it is the *via crucis* of a race and culture considered inferior by their oppressors, the Anglo-Americans, who had already established themselves in the territory in large numbers and who, when this became a state, came in greater numbers, bringing with them all the power of their money, their technology, of the powerful industrial civilization of North America.

New Mexico became a state in 1912. Today, after half a century: who are they, what are the New Mexicans of Hispanic origin? They are the peons, the laborers, the servants, the wage earners, the straw-bosses, and many of them the worshippers of the Anglo-American conquerors. They are the inferior caste, they are a people who are strangers in their own land. It is strange that it has been necessary to amend the very Constitution of the state, adding to it Article XII, Section 10, so that it reads in part as follows: "The children of Spanish descendance in the state of New Mexico shall never be deprived of the right and privilege of admission and attendance in the schools or other educational institutions of the state and shall never be segregated in separate schools." I repeat now the words that I wrote to my distinguished friend Don Luis Ferré in a public letter, October 6, 1964: "God save the children of Puerto Rico from the day when they have to be protected from discrimination practiced against them by people of alien origin in the schools of their own land!"[12]

9

PUERTO RICANS IN THE UNITED STATES

MANY PUERTO RICANS have left their own land and their own schools to live in other places. Puerto Rican people have lived within the continental United States at least since the mid-1800s, when Puerto Rican revolutionaries, sometimes in exile from their island home, and Cuban patriots joined forces in New York City to organize their rebellions against Spain. Ramón Betances, leader of the ill-fated Lares uprising, and Eugenio María de Hostos, who later founded the League of Patriots, were two of the most famous Puerto Ricans who used New York City as a base for the island's fight for independence from Spain.

Also during the nineteenth century, *criollo* families of some wealth began to send their sons to the United States to be educated; perhaps because they wanted to loosen their ties with Spain and Europe; or because their fortunes were closely linked to the growing commerce between Puerto Rico and the United States; or simply because the United States was closer.

Another element entered the immigration picture almost as soon as the United States took possession of Puerto Rico: an element which has had major consequences and which more than anything else accounts for the fact that today over one million Puerto Ricans live in the United States. To an extent that is rarely given adequate recognition, the great industrial and agricultural development of the United States has always required a large supply of cheap labor. It did not take long for Anglo-American developers to make the Puerto Rican population a part of the labor pool of the United States. In 1900 and 1901 more than six thousand Puerto Rican sugar-cane workers were contracted to work in the sugar fields of Hawaii—another newly acquired United States island possession (1898). The Puerto Ricans were shipped by boat to New York, then by train to San Francisco, and again by boat to Hawaii. Considering the distance and the awkwardness of travel, it does not seem surprising that the majority of those Puerto Ricans remained in Hawaii.

Records of Puerto Rican migration to and from the United States have been kept by the U.S. Immigration and Naturalization Service since 1908. These records support the contention that Puerto Ricans have left their homes and come to the United States because they were needed by continental industry and agriculture. A Columbia University study made in 1948 which correlated the year by year figures of Puerto Rican migration with the ups and downs of the mainland business cycle computed the coefficient of correlation at 0.73. According to professors of sociology Clarence Senior and Donald O. Watkins, that figure represents "an exceedingly high correlation for any two series of social statistics."

Because of a prevalent myth that Puerto Ricans flock to the United States whenever times are bad on the island, or that they come to swell the numbers of unemployed and add to the welfare rolls, this point becomes important. To quote from the study ("Toward a Balance Sheet of Puerto Rican Migration") prepared by Professors Senior and Watkins in 1965 for the United States – Puerto Rico Commission on Status:

> . . . the evidence is overwhelming that the vast majority of the Puerto Ricans who come to the United States came because they were needed in the economic machinery of the areas to which they went and they went when they were needed. A few years ago, for example, the economist for the local utility company in New York City estimated that about three million of the city's eight million inhabitants depended, directly or indirectly, on the needle trades for a livelihood. And the Harvard study of the economy of the New York metropolitan region found the needle trades and other industries heavily dependent on the Puerto Rican migrant for a reliable and capable supply. It reported that: "The rate of Puerto Rican migration to New York is one of the factors that determine how long and how successfully the New York metropolitan region will re-

tain industries which are under competitive pressure from other areas. To the extent that some of these industries have hung on in the area, they have depended on recently arrived Puerto Rican workers. . . ."[1]

Assuming that the Harvard University people know what they are talking about, it would seem that many non-Puerto Ricans in the New York area owe their jobs to the Puerto Rican workers, for of the three million people dependent on the needle trades certainly the majority are not Puerto Rican.

Overall, when the demand for workers in the United States goes up, net migration from Puerto Rico goes up along with it; when the need for labor goes down, the net migration from Puerto Rico slows down—and even, sometimes, reverses itself so that more Puerto Ricans return to the island than those who leave it. Specific examples at the local level are numerous, as well. For example, in early 1953 there were about three thousand Puerto Ricans living in Youngstown, Ohio. Then Youngstown was affected by the recession; by early 1954 there were only nine hundred Puerto Ricans in Youngstown. Most of the others had returned to Puerto Rico. Then a few years later the need for workers in Youngstown began to rise again, and by 1960 the Puerto Rican population had increased again to nearly two thousand.

The total numbers of Puerto Ricans involved in moving to and from the United States has, of course, increased markedly during the years since the occupation of Puerto Rico by the United States. Between 1909 and 1930 net migration to the United States averaged less than two thousand persons yearly. During the depression years of the 1930s the number dropped to less than one thousand. In 1940 the number began to rise, averaging more than 18,000 yearly for the decade. The rise continued as the postwar years' boom in the United States continued to create an increasing demand for workers and as lowered air fares and decreased flight times made it easier for Puerto Ricans to get to where the jobs were. Net migration to the United States hit its peak year in 1953, with a figure of more than 69,000. The recession that hit the United States economy that year reduced migration to about 21,500 in 1954. For all of the 1950s, the yearly average was 41,000. During the 1960s there were three years when more Puerto Ricos returned to the island than came to the United States: 1961, 1963, and 1969. In 1970 there was a surge; in 1971 net migration was down to less than 2,000 persons.

Rather than continue with an examination of statistics, we will simply note that by far the majority of Puerto Ricans in the United States are in New York and New Jersey, with the third largest concentration living in Illinois. A majority of new arrivals in Puerto Rico left a job to come to the United States, and in the United States have found jobs at a higher rate of pay. The majority of them have found jobs that are unskilled or semiskilled, yet they have consistently sent money back to Puerto Rico. In 1963, for example (last year for which a specific figure is available), $66 million in personal remittances were sent to the island by Puerto Ricans in the United States.

Obviously, the extreme poverty that has been prevalent in Puerto Rico has been a real factor in the migration of Puerto Rican workers. In addition to whatever motives of adventure, desire to be with relatives who have already migrated, or hope of better education for their children they may have, most Puerto Ricans who emigrate do so in search of a better economic life. If the needle trades in New York City are in need of cheap labor they don't have much success recruiting, for example, in Nassau County, New York, where the median family income in 1960 was $6,665. But even after the years of remarkable economic improvement achieved by Puerto Rico since World War II, personal income is substantially lower than the average in any state. So even the low-scale wages paid by some industries in the United States have allowed them to draw upon the Puerto Rico labor pool. But even though Puerto Rican workers in the United States may be earning more than they would in Puerto Rico, the chances are that within the mainland city or community where they live and work they will be among the poorest in the community. In New York City, for example, that means that they will very likely live in one of the slum or ghetto areas, such as East Harlem, for there is little opportunity for gracious living in New York City if one is poor. Poverty cannot be glorified anywhere, but it certainly does not enhance the experience to have to endure it in an East Harlem tenement.

A booklet titled *Emigración*, published by the Puerto Rican Department of Public Education to provide some orientation for prospective emigrants, has this to say, for example, on the subject of housing:

> New York has 8,000,000 inhabitants. The population keeps growing, but the necessary houses are not built. The government develops new housing projects. But they are not enough.
>
> The problem of housing in New York is worse for the Puerto Ricans. Why? Because the Puerto Rican who emigrates is almost always the poor Puerto Rican. He must look for cheap apartments. And cheap apartments almost cannot be found. There are cheap apartments only in the worst areas. And in those areas the buildings are very old, very damp and full of rats. Buildings that almost never have heat. Buildings which many times should be closed up by the health department. And in many cases the poor Puerto Rican who arrives in the city will be left with no choice but to go ahead and live in that kind of undesirable building.
>
> The apartments, besides, be they better or worse, are always small. Why? For two reasons: because there is little space available and because *American families have few children*. Those small apartments give a tight, closed-in feeling. A person who has lived in the country, with the *batey* at his door, may be very bothered by that confinement. It takes a long time for one to get used to that type of housing.

Also, in New York City it is not usual for many persons to sleep in the same room as we are used to here. Why? Because the ventilation is poor in the winter. Owing to the cold, windows must be kept closed. And a closed room where several persons sleep is bad for the health of all. In the buildings where Puerto Rican workers live there is no place for children to play. There is no patio nor *batey*. If there is a park nearby the children are happy. But if there is none they have to play in the street when they are not in school. And sometimes the advantages of education received in school are wasted by the bad company and bad influences of the street. Education and parents' care of children is more difficult, then, and more complicated for parents in the big cities like New York.

In many of those buildings with cheap rents there is no heat. And to live in a house without heat during the winter is very dangerous for the health of all members of the family.

To make an end, in the United States, as in all places, there are good things. But there is also poverty; there is want; there are discomforts; there are problems; there are dangers; and there are difficulties in living. It is good to know that in order not to suffer unnecessary disappointments.[2]

It may seem that the problem of rotten housing is a problem of the poor rather than the problem of the Puerto Rican. In a sense this is true, for Puerto Rican people are not the only poor in the United States nor are they the only ghetto dwellers. Nor, for that matter, are all Puerto Ricans poor, although the majority of those who come to the United States as immigrating workers are poor. But when a very large percentage of an identifiable group (such as Puerto Ricans) find it especially difficult to get any other than the lowest paying jobs even when their skills should qualify them for better; when they find themselves barred from certain labor unions that have practical monopolies on certain trades for which relatively high wages are the norm; when they find their access to housing outside certain areas limited not only by poverty but by landlords' reluctance to rent to them because of who they are; when it is made more difficult for them to exercise their political rights than it is for other groups within the same social and political system; when they are found to be virtually without political representation, as a group, within the larger society of which they form a part; when their children are put at a disadvantage within an educational system; and when they receive less than their share in quantity or quality of public and social services — then that group is suffering from more than poverty, it is suffering from discrimination. In those United States cities where they constitute a large segment of the population, Puerto Ricans as a class suffer from these things.

It is significant that the booklet *Emigración* has a section titled "What is Prejudice?" Taking first the example of Jews and Blacks, this orientation booklet for Puerto Rican emigrants rather gently defines prejudice as people's habit of blaming a whole group for the actions of a few of its members. Then it warns: "Well all right, the same thing

that happens to Jews and Blacks may happen to
Puerto Ricans in the United States." But the gentle
description of how prejudice occurs and is motivated does not blind the booklet's author to the
consequences of that prejudice. Puerto Ricans are
made to pay for other people's prejudices, he says.
How? "We pay because a bad opinion may be
formed of us. And the result can be that we are
slandered, we are not given work, or we are denied our rights." Not every *americano* is preju-
diced, of course—the writer continues—and Puerto Ricans should not judge all of them by what
some of them do to Puerto Ricans, but: "We ought
to be alert against prejudice so that injustices are
not done to us."

The section on prejudice concludes as follows:

There have been Puerto Ricans who have been cow-
ardly in the face of prejudice in the United States. And
their solution to the problem has been to believe in the
prejudices of some Americans. There is nothing more
terrible than to see a Puerto Rican in the United States
contaminated by its prejudices. That Puerto Rican be-
gins by attacking Black Americans and ends by attacking
his own Puerto Rican brothers. That kind of *boricua* be-
trays his own and goes so far as to deny that he is Puerto
Rican. That kind of wrongly "Americanized" *boricua* is
one of the Puerto Ricans' worst enemies. We must be
alert in order not to fall into that terrible error.[3]

The "prejudice" discussed in the Puerto Rican
booklet mentioned above is also discussed by Professors Senior and Watkins, specifically as it was
manifested in the legislation of the 1920s passed to

keep the United States free of alien races.

Ethnocentrism is a generalized emotional feeling that one's own group knows the correct and only really moral ways of living and that "strangers," with different manners and morals, are inferior. . . . Xenophobia, the pathological extension of ethnocentrism, is defined by psychiatrists as a "morbid fear of strangers." The combination of ethnocentrism and xenophobia which has most often expressed itself in the United States is racist feeling, the idea that it is the so-called "white" race which has made the only contribution of any value to the building of civilization. It easily gets confused with religion, social customs, manners, dress, personal habits, and other matters which are no way intrinsically related to race.

Racism, a witches' brew of false analogies between animal and plant genetics and human inheritance, of spurious reasoning from the mythical history of a non-existent "Nordic race," of Brahmin endeavor to maintain social status, of misinterpreted Darwinism, and of amateurish anthropology, flavored with wartime hysteria and postwar xenophobia, was written into the Federal statutes by the national origin and quota laws. . . . The Immigration and Naturalization Service "Monthly Review" pointed out in January 1947 that: "In its broader sense the National Origins Plan was intended to preserve the racial composition of the United States through the selection of immigrants from those countries whose traditions, language, and political systems were akin to those in this country."[4]

When those laws were passed, Puerto Rico was already an "unincorporated territory" of the United States and its citizens were also United States citizens. And as it happened, they were useful additions to the labor force needed in the United States. But the racism and "morbid fear of strangers" that made Anglo-Americans pass laws against black- and brown-skinned people of Africa, India, etc., was not blind to the color of many Puerto Ricans whose blood heritage included that of Africa and of Taíno Boriquén. The racism described above, and in so many other studies made for governmental commissions inquiring into the social problems of the United States, has been, and is, one of the facts of life for Puerto Ricans who have come to live and work in the "white America" of the United States—of which they are citizens.

Anglo-Americans have earned a broad reputation for their unwillingness to accept any language other than their own. Ambassadors from the United States to other countries have hardly ever had a command of those countries' languages; United States government and even business employees stationed abroad for years seem to pride themselves on not having spoken a word of anything but English; tourists expect to be served in English by every shopkeeper, taxi driver, hotel clerk, bank teller, and telephone operator they encounter abroad. And in their own country, Anglo-Americans are generally not inclined to be tolerant of those who don't speak English.

Many Puerto Ricans arrive in the United States with little or no knowledge of English, and must cope with the racist attitudes that exist toward them with the handicap of a language barrier. In New York City ghetto areas stories about the

"English lessons" administered by police to Puerto Rican men in precinct houses are common and are usually told by eyewitnesses. The procedure is simple: the Puerto Rican man being "taught" is handcuffed and then interrogated in English. Each time he cannot answer in English the interrogating officer hits him.

A lack of knowledge of the English language, often combined with uncertainty about the laws and procedures of the country, can make Puerto Ricans vulnerable to many attacks that are as brutal in their own way as police-administered "English lessons." Unscrupulous merchants in Puerto Rican neighborhoods can sometimes manage to get a tremendous amount of misinterpretation into their explanation of a credit contract that the Puerto Rican customer cannot read. Landlords, taxi drivers, credit agents, employment agents, salesmen, union representatives, and employers — almost anyone with whom a Puerto Rican must deal — can turn language confusion into a weapon. In *Island in the City*,[5] Dan Wakefield cites as typical of employer devices to cut overhead costs at the expense of Puerto Rican employees the case of a small garment "shop" which promised a guaranteed forty-two-dollar a week wage to its Puerto Rican women employees when it opened, but paid each of them only twenty-nine dollars at the end of the first week. When challenged, the employer said that the other thirteen dollars had been taken out for taxes. Wakefield's book reflects conditions at the end of the 1950s; wages have gone up since then, even in garment sweatshops, but only the numbers have really changed. For many Puerto Rican workers the following description taken from Wakefield's book is still true: certainly in spirit if not in detail.

Most of the non-union shops pay the sewing machine operator a flat rate of thirty-five cents for every garment they finish, no matter how difficult the garment is to make, or how long it takes. The unions, which also work by the piece, have a set scale determined by the contract that rates each garment according to the difficulty of the work, and many garments that a union operator makes for seventy cents or ninety cents still get only thirty-five cents in the non-union shop. But it is part of the method of the sweatshop boss to pay a few of the girls much more highly than the others. There are always a few women who complain and threaten to quit or call in a union. The boss will draw these ladies aside and secretly raise their scale much higher, sometimes double the rate of the other workers. These women then stay quiet and help the boss keep the other workers in line.

The boss also has his own devices for insuring the quiet and uncomplaining work of the other women. Since most of the people who work in such shops have little cash on hand at any time, they furnish their homes and families' needs with installment buying. A credit reference is usually needed and the boss of the sweatshop is only too glad to provide it. He may even loan the women five or ten dollars to help them make the first payment. Then, when the time finally comes, as it did on 125th Street, that a union starts to picket and try to recruit, the boss tells the women that if they join the union or leave the shop he will call the furni-

ture store or the clothing store where he has given his
name as a reference and have everything that the
woman is paying installments on taken away from her.
This often means the entire furnishings of a home.
The women are seldom anxious to test the challenge.[6]

Also in the late 1950s a series of complaints
brought by Puerto Rican workers seeking help
against a number of local labor unions engaged in
collaboration with employers to exploit the members they were supposedly protecting were given
publicity by the Association of Catholic Trade
Unionists. For example:

Local 1648 of the Retail Clerks International
Association, AFL-CIO, signed a contract with
Morgan's Leather Goods and Rudee's Leather
Goods (New York City) as representatives of the
two firms' employees. This was done without the
employees' knowledge or consent. Next the two
firms gave their workers a choice between joining
the union or finding other employment. Two
workers asked to see the contract first; both were
fired. Most employees (average pay forty-two dollars per week) signed cards authorizing the firms
to deduct four dollars monthly from their wages as
union dues.

About six months later, the workers of the two
shops decided to organize their own union. They
formed an Organizing Committee and petitioned
the National Labor Relations Board for an election. In response, employers and union officials,
together, called a meeting and threatened to fire

anyone who refused to pay dues to the "legal" union local. Workers began to picket; the employers went to court to get an injunction against the picketers. The New York Supreme Court refused to find in favor of the employers and so the picketing continued. But not for long; New York City Welfare Department employees escorted strike-breaking workers through the picket lines until the strike was, in fact, broken.

When the ACTU, whose lawyers represented the leather-shop workers in the example just described, testified before the McClellan Committee in 1957, it became clear that this case was almost a commonplace example of the practice of some unions which actively sought to "represent" Puerto Rican workers. These unions agreed to worker conditions set by the employer, collected a fee from him in return for a sell-out contract, and then forced workers to pay dues as well. Workers never saw the contracts; union meetings were never held; worker grievances simply disappeared; and workers were often fired just before they were supposed to collect some contract benefit, such as a pay raise or a paid vacation.

The publicity generated by the McClellan hearings and the ACTU testimony spurred "responsible" union leaders to a flurry of housecleaning. But even in legitimate unions, many Puerto Rican workers say, things are often little better. If union officials won't stand behind a Puerto Rican worker, even when a genuine labor contract exists that empowers the union to take action, what good is it? Puerto Ricans are just about as underrepresented among union organizers and union officials as they are among political officeholders. Racist union officials may be "honest" in a certain legal sense, but they may prove of little help to a Puerto Rican worker who is the victim of racist discrimination. And even a well-meaning official can do little about a grievance when he and the aggrieved have no common language in which either the grievance or recourse might be communicated.

The school problems of children who must attend English-speaking schools without having any knowledge of the English language is obvious. There are about 100,000 such Puerto Rican children in the New York City schools. But this is an area in which the Board of Education has begun to take remedial steps. In 1971 one school, P.S. 155, had a program in which children were taught in Spanish and were taught English as a special subject. In a number of other schools attempts to "recognize" the Spanish language and Puerto Rican culture are being made. The problem seems to be that there are so few teachers who speak Spanish or who know anything about Puerto Rican culture. Yet complaints are often made by qualified Puerto Rican teachers that they are refused positions by review boards who feel that their Spanish accents would handicap their general teaching ability. Though, in 1971, Education Department chancellor Harvey B. Scribner did appoint Marco A.

Hernandez as New York City's first Puerto Rican high school principal.

Faced with such problems and frustrated by the inadequacy of traditional remedies, a new militancy has been growing among Puerto Ricans, especially young and poor ones, in the United States. Angry outbursts, sometimes destructive of the property of those the young Puerto Ricans identify as their exploiters and oppressors, have taken place since 1966. Community action groups have formed to provide day care for the children of working mothers (60 percent of New York's Puerto Rican families on the welfare rolls receive supplementary assistance, which means that the family has a breadwinner who is working but whose income is not sufficient to meet the family needs), to form shopping cooperatives, to carry out rent strikes in order to force landlords to maintain the buildings in which the strikers live, and sometimes to take over vacant buildings whose space is desperately needed by poor families yet whose landlord for some reason prefers letting it stand vacant.

A students' organization, the Puerto Rican Student Union, is active on the city's campuses, demanding a fair presentation of Puerto Rican history and culture, and developing links with the student independence organizations in Puerto Rico, where on March 4, 1970, militant students burned down the ROTC building at the University.

Probably the best known Puerto Rican revolutionary organization in the United States today is the Young Lords party. The Young Lords began in Chicago as a self-defense street gang in the "West Side Story" style. In 1968, after a number of ups and downs and near-dissolutions, the Young Lords reorganized with a greatly increased political and social awareness and soon became embroiled in a struggle for Black and Puerto Rican representation on the Community Conservation Council. The Young Lords organization grew and spread; in New York it was established as the Young Lords party and developed a program of thirteen points which include Puerto Rican independence, self-determination for all Latin Americans, equality of women, and a socialist society. The YLP works to educate Puerto Ricans to the YLP political position, and it works in the Puerto Rican ghettos to provide social services which are needed and which Puerto Ricans say they cannot get from local government agencies. The YLP operates a breakfast program for Puerto Rican children who otherwise would go to school hungry. The YLP has a public health unit through which it does what it can to increase the health care needed by Puerto Ricans. In implementing this service, the YLP took over a mobile X-ray unit in New York City. That action was explained in *La Raza* magazine.

> Because we needed more resources to handle our TB work, we went to hospitals and the New York TB Association to use their X-ray machines. We were constantly refused. To serve our people more fully, we liberated an X-ray truck in the name of Betances. At the

present time, Powers, the company that owns the truck, has taken back all of its trucks (including the city's). Now there are no trucks on the street. Our people realize that even though the action of taking the truck was to provide a service, if we don't play the pig's game, we are told to drop dead.[7]

On June 7, 1970, the new militancy made itself evident for the first time in the Puerto Rican Day Parade down Fifth Avenue. A contingent composed of Young Lords, MPI (*Movimiento Pro Independencia*), and Puerto Rican Student Union marched with the Puerto Rican flag and pictures of Puerto Rican independence heroes such as Betances and Albizu Campos. They were received with cheers and applause.

At another Puerto Rican event in 1970 the YLP and Puerto Rican student representatives were not received as warmly. At the Puerto Rican Convention of New Jersey held in October 1970 at Atlantic City, the militants' position was too radical for the majority. A compromise of sorts was reached by deciding that the "traditional" Puerto Rican leaders would draw up one list of resolutions while the "radicals" drew up their own. The "traditionals," who represented the Puerto Rican population of fifty-three New Jersey towns, drew up a list of more than one hundred resolutions, including demands for rent control, cooperative housing, increased welfare benefits, and bilingual educational programs. The "radical" group's resolutions included a demand for the independence of Puerto Rico and the freeing of all political prisoners.

These groups did not represent specific towns, but a growing attitude of Puerto Rican youth.

On June 13, 1971, the New York City Puerto Rican Day Parade was scheduled once more. This time, the militant groups claimed the right to march at the head of the parade with Puerto Rican poor people because:

> We feel that the parade must reflect the reality of life for us as Puerto Ricans. We are poor, and our island is a colony of the United States—it is controlled by the *yanquis*. For these reasons, we asked that our people, not just the Young Lords Party or the Puerto Rican Student Union, or El Comité, but all poor people, march at the head of the parade.[8]

According to the YLP, the Parade Committee said this was not possible; that the police would march at the head of the parade because that was already a parade tradition.

The parade took place as scheduled, but it erupted into a melee in which fifty Puerto Ricans were injured and twenty were arrested. Thirteen police reported injuries.

According to police authorities, the Puerto Rican militants disrupted the parade's march and attacked police who tried to restore order.

According to the YLP:

> . . . we were assembling in the streets at 59th Street and Fifth Avenue. There were about two thousand Boricuas preparing to march to protest budget cuts [in city government], layoffs, and U.S. control of Puerto Rico. While we were negotiating with the Parade

Committee, police prepared to attack us. When we saw this, we tried to move people on to the sidewalks, but the police were out for blood. They charged into us with clubs swinging.[9]

Charges and countercharges have been made as to who was responsible for the disturbance. Puerto Ricans charged police brutality; police called the charge false. But the *New York Times* did publish a photograph the next day showing several policemen who appeared to be beating a Puerto Rican man who lay on the sidewalk. One of the police officers had in his hand a piece of two-by-four board about three feet long.

In late summer of 1971 a series of violent outbreaks took place in New Jersey, involving confrontations between Puerto Rican youths and police officers. In Hoboken, two nights of angry demonstration, window-smashing, and clashes with police followed an eye-witness's report that police were beating two Puerto Rican brothers, Luis and Jaime Santana, whom police accused of assaulting a merchant with a knife in the course of a holdup attempt. Outraged Puerto Ricans demonstrated in front of the police headquarters and the demonstration turned into a confrontation. In the trouble that followed, thirty-five Puerto Ricans were arrested, but were ultimately released as part of an agreement that ended the eruption. An undetermined number of Puerto Ricans were injured, and the police claimed nine injuries.

The truce between Puerto Ricans and police in Hoboken was reached on September 6. Less than two weeks later the Puerto Rican Convention of New Jersey held its second annual meeting in Atlantic City. Hector S. Rodríguez, director of the convention, was interviewed by the press about the recent conflicts in the state. He said that almost none of the resolutions passed by the convention of the year before had been acted upon, and said also that this year the convention would outline a plan for more direct action. In contrast to the 1970 convention, which was addressed by New Jersey Governor William Cahill, the 1971 convention invited no public officials. Inasmuch as the State of New Jersey had no Puerto Rican elected official at any level of government, Puerto Ricans in 1971 invited no politicians to their convention, which reflects a major break with "traditional" hopes for resolving problems by enlisting the participation of officials who are inside the system.

The press had questions also as to how the convention would regard the participation of the YLP and other "radical" groups after the disagreements of the year before. Rodríguez answered that he expected and encouraged their attendance. As to the violence of the past weeks, Rodríguez took the point of view that the 1970 convention should have been sufficient notice of the growing militancy and frustration among New Jersey's Puerto Ricans.

Especially at this time, a book on Puerto Rico

cannot be finished; it can only end. There is a pro-statehood governor in Puerto Rico; there is growing militancy both in the United States and in the island to bring independence finally to Puerto Rico. The economic difficulties of the United States are being felt—as they have always been since the United States tied the island to its economic apron strings—even more acutely in Puerto Rico. The prospects for either statehood or independence seem as confused as ever, but there seems to be an increasing weariness with Commonwealth which, in spite of great efforts by the Puerto Rican government that engineered it, has never been able to be presented convincingly as permanent. In Puerto Rico, 1972 will be an election year, and politicking on the island is heavy. Perhaps the sense of crisis reflects reality and will result in some final resolution of the problems Puerto Rico has struggled with for so long; perhaps, again, some compromise will be reached which may not finally resolve anything, but which will ease the present strains.

But one thing does seem reasonable. To paraphrase Hector S. Rodríguez's bitter complaint, it does seem high time that real notice be taken of the growing militancy and frustration among the people of Puerto Rico.

NOTES

Chapter 1:

1 Casas, Bartolome de la., Bp. of Chiapa 1474–1566. *Historia de las Indias*. Edicion de Agustin Millares Carlo y estudio preliminar de Lewis Hanke. Mexico, Fondo de Cultura Economica, 1951. 3 vols.

2 Cruz Monclova, Lidio. "The Puerto Rican Political Movement in the 19th Century." In *Status of Puerto Rico*, Selected Background Studies prepared for the U.S.–Puerto Rican Commission on the Status of Puerto Rico, 1966, p. 2.

Chapter 3:

1 Lewis, Gordon K. *Puerto Rico: Freedom and Power in the Caribbean*. New York: MR Press, 1963, p. 1.

2 Vivas, José Luis. *The History of Puerto Rico*. New York: Las Americas Publishing Co., 1970, p. 100.

Chapter 5:

1 Cruz Monclova, op. cit, p. 6.

2 Cruz Monclova, op. cit, p. 15.

3 Cruz Monclova, op. cit, pp. 19–20.

4 Cruz Monclova, op. cit, p. 21.

5 Vivas, op. cit., p. 139.

6 Vivas, op. cit., p. 265.

7 Vivas, op. cit., p. 150.

8 Maria Cristina's Royal Decree of 11/25/1897. Reprinted in *Documents on the Constitutional History of Puerto Rico.*, second ed. Office of the Commonwealth of Puerto Rico, Washington, D.C. 1964, p. 45.

Chapter 6:

1 General Miles's Proclamation in *Documents on the Constitutional History, etc.*, p. 55.

2 *Documents* op. cit., pp. 56–57.

3 Vivas, op. cit., p. 183.

4 Treaty of Paris, Article IX in *Documents*, op. cit., p. 50.

5 Lewis, op cit.

6 Circular issued by Commanding Brigadier General George W. Davis, in *Documents*, op. cit., pp. 59–63.

7 Carroll, Henry K. "Report on the Island of Porto Rico," Washington: US Govt. Printing Office, 1899, p. 57.

8 Hunter, Robert J. "Historical Survey of the Puerto Rico Status Question, 1898–1965." In *Status of PR*, op. cit., p. 73–74.

9 de Diego, José and Coll y Cuchi, José. *Discursos* (see full citation in Bibliography).

10 Hunter, op. cit., p. 77.

11 Cannon letter in *New York Times*, April 19, 1919, p. 3.

12 Letter from Horace M. Towner to the P.R. legislature in *La Democracia* (San Juan), March 8, 1921.

13 Gov. E. Montgomery Reily, inaugural speech, 1921. *La Democracia* (San Juan) July 31, 1921.

14 Letter from Reily to Antonio Barceló. *La Democracia* (San Juan), February 13, 1922.

Chapter 7:

1 Muñoz Marín, Luis. "Porto Rico: The American Colony," pp. 373–393 in *These United States, A Symposium*, Second Series, Gruening, Ernest. ed. New York: Boni & Liveright, 1925.

2 Wells, Henry. *The Modernization of Puerto Rico*, Cambridge, Mass.: Harvard University Press, 1929, p. 92.

3 Wagenheim, Kal. *Puerto Rico: A Profile*, p. 78. New York: Praeger, 1970.

4 Lewis, op. cit., p. 92.

5 Hunter, op. cit., p. 96.

6 Vivas, op. cit, p. 240.

7 Medina Ramirez, Ramón. *El Movimiento Libertador en la Historia de Puerto Rico*. Santurce: Puerto Rico Printing and Publishing Co., Inc., 1954, p. 195.

8 Mahoney. U.S. Congress Senate Hearings, 82nd Congress, second session, April 29, 1952, p. 19.

9 U.S. Congress. Public Law 447–82nd Congress, Chapter 567–second session, H.J. Res. 430, Joint Resolution, All 66 Stat. 327. In *Documents* op. cit., p. 195.

Chapter 8:

1 Rodríguez Bou (see Bibliography), p. 161.

2 Rodríguez Bou, op. cit, pp. 159–160.

3 Cebollero, Pedro A., "A School Language Policy for Puerto Rico." Superior Educational Council, Series II, No. 1. San Juan: Casa Baldrich, Inc., 1945.

4 Rodríguez Bou, op. cit., p. 161.

5 Osuna, Juan José, *A History of Education in Puerto Rico*, pp.

376–377. Rio Piedras: Editorial de la Universidad de Puerto Rico, 1949.

6 Osuna, pp. 392–395.

7 *Public Education and the Future of Puerto Rico: A Curriculum Survey.* Institute of Field Studies, Teachers College, Columbia Univ., NY, 1949 as quoted in Bou, op. cit.

8 Wagenheim, op. cit., p. 122.

9 Wagenheim, op. cit., p. 229.

10 Rodríguez Bou, p. 199.

11 Rodríguez Otero, Eladio. *La Personalidad Cultural de Puerto Rico y el Status Político*, pp. 15–16. Unpublished position paper presented to the Puerto Rican Commission on the Status of Puerto Rico. San Juan, 1965. Gift to the Columbia University Library.

12 Rodríguez Otero, pp. 22–24.

Chapter 9:

1 Senior, Clarence and Watkins, Donald O. "Toward a Balance Sheet of Puerto Rican Migration." In *Status of Puerto Rico*, Selected Background Studies, etc., pp. 704–705.

2 Division de Educacion de la Comunidad, Departamento de Instruccion Publica. *Emigración*. Segunda Edicion, San Juan, 1966, pp. 63–65.

3 *Emigración*, pp. 50–57.

4 Senior and Watkins, p. 693.

5 Wakefield, Dan. *Island in the City*. Boston: Houghton Mifflin Co., 1959, pp. 205–207.

6 Wakefield, p. 202.

7 *La Raza*, Vol. I, No. 2, Los Angeles, Calif., p. 87.

8 *What Happened at the Parade?* Leaflet, Young Lords party, June 1971.

9 Ibid.

BIBLIOGRAPHY

(With a few exceptions, books and articles included in the Notes section are not repeated here.)

American Academy of Political and Social Science. *Puerto Rico: A Study of Democratic Development.* Philadelphia, 1953.

Arce de Vazquez, Margot. *La Obra Literaria de José de Diego.* San Juan: Instituto de Cultura Puertorriqueña, 1967.

Baer, Werner. *The Puerto Rican Economy and United States Economic Fluctuations.* Río Piedras: Social Science Research Center (University of Puerto Rico), 1962.

Berbusse, Edward J., S.J. *The U.S. in Puerto Rico, 1898–1900.* Chapel Hill: University of North Carolina Press, 1966.

Blanco, Tomás. *El Prejuicio Racial en Puerto Rico.* San Juan: Editorial Biblioteca de Autores Puertorriqueños, 1942.

Coll y Cuchi, José. *Un Problema América.* Mexico: Editorial Jus, 1944.

D'Estefano, Miguel A. *Puerto Rico: Analysis of a Plebiscite.* Havana: Tricontinental, 1968.

de Diego, José and Coll y Cuchi, José. *Discursos Pronunciados en Santo Domingo con motivo del Dia de la Raza, por José de*

Diego en 1915 y por José Coll y Cuchi en 1923. Third Edition. Printed in New York, 1928.

Diaz Soler, Luis M. *Historia de la Esclavitud Negra en Puerto Rico.* Universidad de Puerto Rico: Editorial Universitaria, 1970.

Fernandez Mendez, Eugenio. *La Identidad y la Cultura.* San Juan: Ediciones "El Cemi," 1959.

Géigel Polanco, Vicente. *El Despertar de un Pueblo.* San Juan: Biblioteca de Autores Puertorriqueños, 1942.

Glass, Alex, ed. *Puerto Rico Living, The Complete Guide for Persons Living, Working or Doing Business in the Puerto Rican Commonwealth.* Vol 9, No. 1, San Juan: Living, Inc., 1971.

Handlin, Oscar. *The Newcomers, Negroes and Puerto Ricans in a Changing Metropolis.* Cambridge, Mass: Harvard University Press, 1959.

Hunter, Robert J. *Puerto Rico, A Survey of Historical, Economic, and Political Affairs.* Committe on Interior and Insular Affairs, House of Representatives, 11/25/59. Washington, D.C.: U.S. Government Printing Office, 1959.

Jaffe, A. J.. *People, Jobs and Economic Development.* Glencoe, Illinois: Free Press, 1959.

Lewis, Oscar. *La Vida.* New York: Random House, 1965.

Mathews, Thomas. *Puerto Rican Politics and the New Deal.* Gainesville: University of Florida Press, 1960.

Mikesell, Raymond F. *Promoting U.S. Private Investment Abroad.* Planning Pamphlet No. 101, Oct. 1957, National Planning Association, Washington, D.C.

Mills, C. Wright, Clarence Senior, and Rose Kohn Goldsen. *The Puerto Rican Journey.* New York: Harper, 1950.

Miranda, Luis Antonio. *La Justicia Social en Puerto Rico.* San Juan: Talleres de "La Correspondencia," 1943.

Morales Carrión, Arturo. "Origenes de las Relaciones entre los Estados Unidos y Puerto Rico, 1700–1815." *Historia*, Río Piedras: Universidad de Puerto Rico. Vol. II, April, 1952, pp. 3–50.

Morales Otero, Pablo. *Neustros Problemas*. San Juan: Biblioteca de Autores Puertorriqueños, 1958.

Movimiento Pro-Independencia. *Tesis Politica: La Hora de la Independencia*. San Juan: Editorial Claridad, 1964.

Pedreira, Antonio S. *Insularismo*. San Juan: Biblioteca de Autores Puertorriqueños, 1942.

Perloff, Harvey S. *Puerto Rico's Economic Future, A Study in Planned Development*. Chicago: University of Chicago Press, 1950.

Reuter, Edward Byron. "Culture Contacts in Puerto Rico." *The American Journal of Sociology*, Sept. 1946, Vol. LII, No. 2.

Rodríguez Bou, Ismael. "Significant Factors in the Development of Education in Puerto Rico" in *Status of Puerto Rico*. Selected Background Studies prepared for the U.S.–Puerto Rican Commission on the Status of Puerto Rico, 1966, pp. 147–314.

Senior, Clarence. *Americans All: Our Citizens from the Caribbean*. New York: McGraw Hill, 1965.

Steward, Julian H., Robert A. Manners, Eric. R. Wolf, Elena Padilla Seda, Sidney W. Mintz, Raymond I.. Scheele. *The People of Puerto Rico, A Study in Social Anthropology*. Urbana, Ill.: University of Illinois Press, 1969.

Thomas, Piri. *Down These Mean Streets*. New York: Alfred A. Knopf, 1967.

Tugwell, Rexford Guy. *The Stricken Land*. Garden City, N.Y.: Doubleday & Co., 1947.

INDEX

Abercromby, Sir Ralph, 74–75
absentee ownership, 146–147
Acosta, José Julián, 101, 103–
104
African, first, 16–17
agregados, defined, 94, 135
Agueybana the Elder, receives
Ponce de León, 15–16; wel-
comes Spaniards, 19–20;
dies, 21
Alaska, 175
Albizu Campos, Pedro, leads
Nationalists, 151–152; arrested, 159–160; students support, 169; imprisoned, 171–
172; heroized, 228
America, *see* United States
Americanization, of government
structure, 127–129; economic, 180–181, 200–201; and
politics, 183–184; reaction,
196
Amézquita, Juan de, 58–59

ammunition, 41–42
Antonio de Montesino, Fray,
30–31
Arawak, 4–5
Archaics, 3–4
archeology, 3
Arizmendi, Bishop Juan, 83,
87
army, U.S., 194–195
artisans, 45–47
asiento, 65, 67
assimilation, 95, 105; *see also*
statehood
Autonomous Charter of 1897,
108–111, 131, 177
autonomy, defined, 95; proposed, 97; and Liberal Party,
106; granted, 107; inaugurated, 108–111; frustrated,
111–112; and Spanish American War, 116; and Muñoz
Marín, 168–169; *see also*
Commonwealth